Rossendale United Football Club 1898–2011

A Season by Season History

by

David Andrew Rogan

Grosvenor House
Publishing Limited

The right of David Andrew Rogan to be identified as the author of this
work has been asserted in accordance with Section 78
of the Copyright, Designs and Patents Act 1988

The book cover is copyright to David Andrew Rogan

This book is published by
Grosvenor House Publishing Ltd
Link House
140 The Broadway, Tolworth, Surrey, KT6 7HT.
www.grosvenorhousepublishing.co.uk

A CIP record for this book
is available from the British Library

ISBN 978-1-83975-708-2

Contents

Acknowledgements

Rawtenstall Library

Rossendale Free Press

Bacup Times

Bacup Library

David Howarth

Geoff Pickup

Billy Haworth

Nigel Birch

British Newspaper Archive

Lancashire Evening Telegraph

Foreword

It is 10 years since Rossendale United played their last game a 1-0 win over Maine Road at their historic Dark Lane home watched by just 106 supporters. A club that represented the valley of Rossendale for 112 years enjoying some great highs and many more lows, but always entertained and warmly hosted many people and football clubs from all over the country. Hopefully, this history will honour those who have worked for and represented the club at whatever level and ensure their achievements are not forgotten.

The Early Years 1898–1916

Formation of Rossendale Utd

After the demise of both the Rawtenstall and Rossendale football clubs in 1897 a meeting was called on the 6th July 1898 at the Red Lion Pub, Cloughfold to form a new football club for the Borough of Rawtenstall using the Rossendale clubs former ground Dark Lane. At this meeting it was decided the club should represent the whole of the valley and representations were sent out to the Bacup area whose club had recently folded and left the Lancashire Football League. To this end a further meeting was held at the Royal Hotel and despite the fact that there was no response from the Bacup area it was decided the club should be called Rossendale United and a committee was formed with equal representation from both Rawtenstall and Waterfoot. The following were elected to the committee Messrs. Browning, Edmundson, Billington, Tattersall and Barlow from Rawtenstall and Garside, Kershaw, Haworth, Moore, Barcroft and Ormerod from Waterfoot, with Mr J Stott as secretary, H. Smethurst as Treasurer and Mr R Mitchell as president.

The use of the Dark Lane ground was secured from the current tenant a Mr John Lord who was fully behind the new club and the club entered the North East Lancashire league taking over the fixtures of the now defunct Rawtenstall club, it was also decided to enter the English FA Cup and the Lancashire Junior Cup. All that was needed now was a team although with junior football going from strength to strength in the valley the club's trainer former Everton and Rossendale player Johnny Weir thought a decent side could be got together with one or two additions from the surrounding area.

David Ashworth original committee member who went on to manage Oldham, Liverpool and Man City amongst others.

Joseph Stott first secretary of Rossendale United.

The First season 1898–99

The season opened with home game against Oswaldtwistle Rovers and a crowd of around 2000 witnessed a fine 3-1 win, Jack Read scoring the first goal for the club. There followed a 3-0 defeat against a strong Nelson reserve side and draw with Earby before Rossendale travelled to Workington for their first game in the FA Cup. The team left Waterfoot station on the 5,30am train to Bury and had to change trains five times before reaching Workington at 2.00pm and the long journey meant the club fielded a weakened team, including trainer Weir to make up the numbers and eventually lost 3-1.

The club also suffered defeat in the Lancashire Junior Cup losing 2-0 at local rivals Haslingden. The club however showed reasonable form in the league and by the beginning of December had won four lost four and drawn two of their ten league games. However, the late arrival of the opposition has seen gates dwindle from their promising opening with only a few hundred witnessing the games.

The withdrawal of Darwen reserves from the Lancashire Combination saw the Rossendale club invited to take over their fixtures and the committee gladly accepted the challenge.

The club found the step up in standard difficult and opened with a 5-0 drubbing at Manchester City reserves and only two more games were won against Blackburn Park Road and Hurst Ramblers, although home games against the reserve sides of Mancester City, Burnley and Preston boosted gates. The season finished with an 11-1 defeat at Skerton as the club finished in bottom place.

Despite this it was quite a shock given the club had been invited to take over Darwen's fixtures when the club were not re-elected to the Lancashire Combination. Overall, the club used forty one players during the season and leading scorer Billy Hoare moved to Football League club New Brighton for the start of the next season.

1899–1900

The Committee decided to enter the Central Lancashire League for the coming season and put together a much changed squad for the new campaign boosted by the return to football of the experienced former Rawtenstall captain Deucie Halliwell.

The season started inauspiciously with an away trip to Freetown where four players failed to make the journey and a makeshift team, with first choice goalkeeper Tattersall at centre half lost heavily 8-2. The team bounced back with three consecutive wins including a double over local rivals Stacksteads, before a 4-0 reverse at favourites Heywood on New Year's Day with the local paper describing several Rossy players as "looking worse for wear". A run of seven league victories including a 2-1 win over closest rivals Black Lane Temperance saw the club top the table at the beginning of April. The run ended with a 6-2 defeat at Black Lane where injuries, illness and players missing train connections meant Rossy played this game with just eight men, to add insult to injury the Rossy players were stoned by opposition fans as they left the pitch. Rossy won their next match at Heywood West End 3-1 and when news filtered through that Black Lane had lost at Little Lever, the club needed to win one of their last two games to be champions. The club won their last game at Little Lever St Matthews 2-0 to be confirmed as Champions.

The club were presented with the trophy at Little Lever and upon their return to the valley were met by the Boothfold brass band and the team were paraded on waggonette through Rawtenstall and up to Waterfoot with speeches and presentations at several hostelries along the way before ending the night at the Blue Bell Inn.

The club also enjoyed success in cup competitions reaching the semi-finals of the Parks Cup and Rossendale Charity Cup as well as most notably the Lancashire Junior Cup where Earby, Clitheroe, Skerton, Accrington Villa and Prescot were all overcome setting up a semi-final with Blackburn Park

Road. A crowd of over 1500 saw Rossendale held to a 1-1 draw and the club were disappointed they were forced to play the replay at Blackburn on a Thursday evening and crashed to a 7-0 defeat.

The 1898-99 Central Lancashire League Champions

Front row: Heys, Billington, John Ashworth, James Ashworth, E. Palmer (Chairman).

2nd row: Joseph Stott(secretary) Howard, Whithead, Halliwell, Townsend, Ellis.

3rd Row: McLay, McLoughlin, Tattersall, Chatburn, Ashworth(trainer).

Back row: Committee members.

1900-01

With most of last season's squad retained the club were confident of defending their title. The season opened with a disappointing 3-2 defeat to Bolton St Luke's, however they bounced back with a then record 8-0 win over Blackrod. After a 5-1 defeat at Heywood the club were boosted by the return of Billy Hoare and won eight of their next twelve games to firmly establish themselves as favourites to retain their title. However, as the season progressed the withdrawal of several clubs from the league and the subsequent loss of points meant the season ended quite chaotically with some clubs not completing their fixtures. This saw Rossendale finish in third place.

The FA cup saw the club drawn away to Rochdale and a large crowd saw a gritty Rossy lose narrowly 1-0. The club also made early exits in the Parks Cup and the Junior Cup but took the Rossendale Charity Cup seriously, entering strong team to see off Helmshore and holders Newchurch Rovers before beating Rawtenstall Rovers 5-1 in a replay after the first game at Dark Lane had been drawn 1-1, to pick up the clubs second piece of silver ware in their short history. Financially despite some fixtures not being completed the season was a success with a small profit being shown allowing loans of £5 7s 11d to be repaid. The club also decided to apply to re-join the Lancashire Combination for the 1901–02 season and their subsequent election generated much interest in the valley for the coming season.

1901–02

The club retained the core of the successful squad from the previous two years although Captain Ducie Helliwell finally decided to hang up his boots. The club did bring in several players in preparation for the tougher test of the Lancashire Combination, full back J.Higham was signed from Middleton whilst forwards Dempsey from Halliwell and Leyland from Stalybridge Rovers were also added to the squad.

The season opened with a 5-0 reverse at Bury Reserves, but the club bounced back with a 2-1 win over Everton Reserves before a crowd of 2000 at Dark Lane. A run of four defeats followed including an 8-1 thrashing at Anfield by Liverpool Reserves and this saw several new players introduced including half back Jimmy Lucas from Bolton, forwards John Taylor from Wigan County, Lang Morris and Sam Bradley from Chorley, whilst local youngster Billy Barker from Newchurch also impressed when given an opportunity. The club then embarked on a five match unbeaten run including a 3-2 win at Turf Moor over Burnley reserves, followed by 3-2 Win at home over Preston reserves which brought in record receipts of over £28. The team then struggled for consistency over the next few months good results like the 5-0 thrashing of Newton Heath Reserves on New year's Day being mixed with heavy defeats such as 6-1 by Everton reserves and 8-1 by Preston reserves who both gained revenge for their earlier defeats at Dark Lane. The introduction of inside forward Billy Cox from Southport who scored 6 goals in 10 games saw the club finish the season well with home with wins against the reserve sides of Liverpool and Bury to finish in a creditable 10th place on their return to the Lancashire Combination.

The clubs cup campaigns were limited to the Junior Cup and Rossendale Charity Cup, in the Junior Cup the club recorded a record 11-0 win over Great Harwood with Sam Bradley netting five goals, this game saw Rossy keeper Gal Tattersall spend much of the game smoking cigarettes whilst chatting to the fans behind the goal, before taking off his overcoat and venturing forward to thunder a header against the cross bar. In the second round the club were surprisingly beaten 2-0 at Padiham. Rossendale's defence of the Charity Cup was hampered by fixture congestion Haslingden were beaten 1-0 before a scratch team was beaten 4-1 by Rawtenstall Rovers in the semi-final.

The first season back in the Lancashire Combination was also a success off the field as the improved gates especially against the reserve sides of football league clubs saw a surplus of over £50 which was used to repay outstanding loans.

1902–03

The club carried out several ground improvements during the close season including providing a new enclosure under the main grandstand and boards behind the goals. The start to the season was spoilt by a contract dispute with Billy Hoare and although it was resolved two weeks into the season a bad injury shortly after ended his career and left Jimmy Howard as the only player left at the club who played in its first ever game in 1898. The main signings for the start of the season were full back John Whittam from Padiham and winger James Walker.

The season opened with a comfortable 4-0 win at Black Lane Temperance and followed this with a creditable 0-0 draw with defending Champions Man City reserves before a large Dark Lane crowd. However, the team struggled adding just two more wins before December, whilst Jimmy Lucas became the first Rosendale player to be sent off for kicking in the away game against Man City reserves. Wins over Heywood and Man Utd reserves over the Christmas period boosted Rossy's position but a winless run of eleven games saw the team slip into the bottom two. With gates falling the club were unable to resist a bid of £75 from Bury for Billy Cox. The club then brought in full back Sam Hulmes from Newton Heath Athletic and John Byrne, whilst Billy Barker returned to the side and the team finished the season strongly winning five of the last eight games to finish fifteenth seven points clear of bottom club Turton.

The club once again entered the FA Cup and pulled of a fine 2-1 at Padiham in the first qualifying round to earn a trip to Accrington Stanley in the next round who won a tight game 1-0 in front of over 4000 fans at Moorhead. In the Lancashire Junior Cup Brynn Central were beaten 4-2, before the club were beaten 8-3 by Clitheroe Central in the next round.

1903–04

Rossendale continued to strengthen the team during the close season with goalkeeper Bob Arrowsmith, full back Peter Greenhalgh and forward Law Ashworth all signing from Rochdale.

The season opened with a 1-1 draw at Heywood before Nelson were beaten 1-0 at Dark Lane the team turning out in a new strip of blue and white stripes for the first time. The strip was donated by local solicitor and football league official Charles Sutcliffe whose advice and support played a major role in the formation of the club.

Following a 4-1 reverse at Colne the club embarked on a three match winning run to move into the top four. This run saw a crowd of over 4000 at Dark Lane for the visit of Accrington Stanley providing record gate receipts of £56. A series of defeats to the reserve sides of the football league clubs saw the team slide down the table, before a run of three wins over the Christmas period stopped the rot. This inconsistency continued with a run of three defeats being followed by a run of four wins to secure the clubs position in the top half of the table. A run of one win from the last 8 matches saw the club slip back to finish a creditable tenth. The fact that only three of the nine teams above them were not the reserve sides of league clubs caused some debate at the clubs' AGM, as it became clear that to compete with the reserve sides and big spending non-league sides like Accrington Stanley and Nelson the wage bill would have to increase, or the club would have to settle for the role of also ran's.

During the season, the club continued to strive to improve facilities and ran a penny appeal, 7570 of which were collected raising over £30 much of which was spent on new dressing rooms which opened on January 16th for the visit of Blackburn reserves.

The club once again entered the English (FA) Cup beating Oswaldtwistle Rovers 4-0 in the first qualifying round before losing 3-1 at Nelson in the next round. Rossy entered the Lancashire Senior Cup for the first time but bowed out at the first round suffering a heavy 4-1 defeat at Chorley.

1904-05

Several new players were signed prior to the new season, left back James Nightingale arrived from Southport, Dick Harrison arrived after a season in the newly formed Lancashire Combination second division with neighbours Bacup, centre forward Joe Hodgkinson was signed from Nelson and experienced former Man Utd winger Harry Lappin arrived from Grimsby Town. The club also signed powerful full back Billy Cook from Ashton Town but had to wait for him to finish the cricket season with Lancashire before he could appear.

Rossy drew the opening game of the season at Bolton reserves but had to wait until October for their first league win then a run of four defeats saw the club slip to fifteenth and a real threat of relegation. An unbeaten five match run towards the end of the year saw the club pull clear of the relegation places as the team saw the benefits of a settled side with local youngster Raper Stott establishing himself at centre half. A run of four defeats in five games saw the club slip back down the table but an eight match unbeaten run secured safety and a comfortable mid table position, before the season petered out with a run of three defeats that saw the club finish in thirteenth place well clear of relegated clubs Ashton town and St Helens Town.

The club also broke their attendance and receipts record towards the end of the season when a crowd of 4600 turned out for the derby with Nelson giving the club record receipts of £66.

In the FA Cup the club needed a replay and then extra time for the first time in the club's history to overcome Oswaldtwistle Rovers 5-4 in the first qualifying round before losing 2-1 at Chorley in the next round. The Lancashire Senior Cup saw Barrow beaten 1-0 at Dark Lane before they disappointingly bowed out to Earlstown in the next round after a replay.

1905-06

During the close season the club lost three out of contract players to football league clubs, Joe Hodgkinson to Bury, Joe Johnson to Grimsby and Harry Lappin to Clapton Orient. Under the leadership of Chairman Charles Sutcliffe the club were determined to strengthen itself and appointed one person to take charge of team affairs for the first time, local school teacher John Watson who had been a scout for several football league clubs. The new man brought in half backs Tom Brooks from Earlestown and George Heaton from the Bolton League, the experienced winger John Flynn who had league experience at Walsall and Bristol City and was signed from Southern League West Ham Utd and most importantly of all Willie Ingham from Freetown who became one of the clubs best ever forwards.

The season started with two draws but the club lost only one of their first eight games to establish themselves in the top three. In fact, just one more game was lost before the Christmas period as the club established themselves as genuine contenders for the league and with gates averaging over £30 some were surprised when the club accepted a bid of £80 from Bradford City for left back James Nightingale at the beginning of December. A surprise 4-1 defeat at Atherton Church House the Saturday before Christmas heralded a run of just one win in seven games that ended any chance of league glory. The club stopped the rot with a 7-0 victory over Stalybridge Rovers with new singings Tommy Rogers from Newton Le Willows slotting in at the now problematic left back position and ex Burnley centre forward Cornelius Hogan scoring four goals. The club chopped and changed the team in an attempt to recapture early season form but consistency eluded them and they eventually slipped down the table to finish twelfth.

In the FA cup Colne were despatched 7-1 at Dark Lane with Ingham scoring 4 goals before the club lost out surprisingly 2-1 at Oswaldtwistle Rovers in the next round. In the Lancashire Senior Cup Rossy drew 2-2 at Dark Lane against a strong Blackpool side before losing the replay 2-1. On and off the pitch the season was deemed a success, inside forward Willie Ingham became the first Rossendale player to score over 20 league goals in a season as he finished with a club record 27 goals in all competitions whilst improved gates and transfer fees saw the club turn a profit of £50 for the season.

1906-07

Preseason saw extensive work done on the ground, the pitch was partially re-laid, the dressing rooms refurbished a new secretary's office provided along with covered accommodation for the gatemen. The club had lost goalkeeper Arrowsmith, Harrison, Barker and Ashworth to local rivals Bacup who had ambitions to win promotion to the Lancashire Combination first division. The experienced Fred McGregor signed towards the end of the previous season from Accrington Stanley was established as first choice keeper whilst inside forward Tommy Becton formerly of Preston and Sunderland arrived from Colne along with Alf Berry from Bury and Harold Dawson from Atherton Church House.

The season did not start well with two defeats in the first three games before wins over Atherton and Liverpool Reserves gave hope, however the next 5 games were lost to send Rossy to the foot of the table. Former Man Utd forward George Lyons was signed from Oldham to stop the rot. Two wins and a draw at the beginning of December saw the club rise to fifteenth. A 2-0 win over Man City reserves on Christmas Day started a twelve match unbeaten run that lifted the club into the top half of the table and ended any relegation fears. However, the last twelve games yielded just one win as the team slipped down to finish thirteenth. The situation not helped by the loss of winger Dawson for the rest of the season after he caught pneumonia playing in atrocious conditions at Accrington Stanley in March and the departure of Cook to play cricket at the beginning of April.

Rossy enjoyed their best FA cup run to date defeating Nelson 3-2 at Seedhill in front of over 4000 fans in the preliminary round, before beating Kirkham 5-0 goalkeeper McGregor scoring from the penalty spot. In the second qualifying round Colne were held to 2-2 draw before Rossy won the replay 8-0 a record FA Cup win for the club. Rossendale then lost a tight game at Southport 1-0 in the next round. The cup run was not without controversy, the club chartered a train to take supporters to the Colne game but only sold 240 of the 300 seats available making a loss, the fallout from this leading to the resignation of club treasurer Robert Taylor and committeeman Walter Heys. There was also a dispute after the Southport game the club lodging a protest about the eligibility of Southport left back Dean which the FA threw out. The Lancashire Senior Cup also brought the club some success St Helens Recs and Accrington Stanley both being beaten after replays the latter 7-1 at Dark Lane to set up a quarter final tie at Anfield against the mighty Liverpool. Unfortunately, the reigning Division one champions proved too strong winning 6-0. Overall, despite a disappointing finishing league position the season could be judged a success Ingham once again topped the 20 goal mark with 26 in all competitions and was joined by Alf Berry with 20. Gates were also up with record receipts of over £76 being recorded for the visit of Accrington Stanley in the league, whilst the visit of Champions elect Oldham also saw a 4000 plus gate and receipts of £72.

1907-08

Off the field there was some reorganisation at the club as Chairman C E Sutcliffe had to stand down due to his increasing commitments at the Football League and Lancashire FA, he was replaced as Chairman by H J Marshall whilst John Watson remained as secretary team selection was once again done by committee with Johnny Weir remaining as trainer. The new FA rule that all players had to be insured also prompted the club to become a Limited Liability company with 100 shares issued at 10 shillings each with ownership limited to just 50 people. This season saw the club produce a match day programme for the first time.

The club had retained most of last season's squad with only Tom Rogers who was sold to Liverpool for a club record £100 and George Lyons who signed for Salford departing. Rogers was replaced at left back by promising amateur John Canon Bardsley from Southport YMCA, whilst winger Alec Jones from Chorley replaced Lyons. The club got off to their best start so far winning their first four games to lie second behind leaders Everton reserves. Some excellent football meant the club stayed in the top four and the club continued to strengthen the team bringing in centre half Arthur Evans from Belfast Distillery and forward John Hall from Turton. Heavy defeats to leaders Everton Reserves home and away meant they were never close to top spot but a 1-0 victory at fellow contenders Carlisle Utd on Boxing Day saw the club finish the year in second place. A shock 3-1 reverse at Southport on New Years Day started a slump of five defeats in the next seven games as the club slipped to sixth, the sale of star full back Billy Cook to Oldham for a new record £200 fee did not help defensively. The return to the club of Dick Harrison from Bacup who bagged 14 goals in the last twelve league games ensured a decent finish to the season and a league best finish of fifth 16 points behind Champions Everton reserves.

In the FA cup Brierfield Swifts were hammered 7-1 in the preliminary round but the next round at Southport proved to be a disaster as four players missed their train connection and the team were forced to start the tie with eight men, by the time the missing players arrived Rossy were 2-0 down, a deficit they were unable to reverse. In the Lancashire Senior Cup the club made the long trip to Barrow only to lose 1-0. The club entered the Rossendale Charity Cup again and fielded strong sides beating Shawforth 1-0 in the semi-final and Bacup 2-0 in the final to lift the trophy for a second time, although this was shrouded in controversy as Rossy were awarded the trophy as Bacup refused to play the second half when trailing 2-0 due to inclement weather conditions.

Despite enjoying a highly successful season gates receipts had decreased slightly and an increased wage bill meant the new Chairman James McLay announced a loss of £27 for the season.

A Rossendale team photo from 1907–08 season with soon to depart Billy Cook 4th from left next to Willie Ingham 3rd left on back row and Raper Stott seated on the left of middle row and trainer Johnny Weir seated on the right. Inset is former Chairman C E Sutcliffe who was to go on to be secretary of the Football League.

1908-09

The main player movement saw Dick Harrison follow former secretary Bert Stansfield to Carlisle where he had been appointed manager, whilst left winger James Whittaker was signed from Clapton Orient on his return north.

The season opened with a 6-1 win at Colne and four wins in the first 6 games saw the club handily placed in sixth, but it was to be December before the club won again by which time the club had slipped to fifteenth and with four teams to be relegated were in a relegation scrap. The club lost leading amateur Bardsley to Everton and replaced him with Harry Rishton from Ramsbottom and brought in forward Lol Cook brother of Billy from Southport.

A Christmas double over Bury reserves lifted the club to eleventh but a six match winless run dragged them back down to fourteenth. With any team in the bottom half of the table in danger of relegation vital wins over Nelson and Blackpool reserves kept Rossy clear of the relegation places. The club struggled to string results together and a 6-0 defeat at Liverpool reserves where keeper McGregor was badly injured and out for the season saw the club drop to sixteenth just above Colne who visited Dark Lane on Good Friday. A crowd of nearly 4000, the biggest of the season turned up for a tense game that Colne won 1-0 to send Rossy into the relegation places for the first time. A surprise 4-2 win over Accrington the following day gave some hope but the last three games were all lost as the club finished in eighteenth place four points off safety to be relegated for the first time in the clubs history.

The cups offered little respite in the FA Cup Fleetwood were beaten 2-1 in the preliminary round to set up a plumb home tie against local rivals Accrington Stanley a record gate of over 4500 giving receipts of £81, turned up to see Stanley win 2-0. In the Lancashire Senior Cup a creditable draw at Bloomfield Rd brought Blackpool to Dark Lane but the game was spoilt when Rossy player Alf Pearson who had just been signed from Blackpool broke his leg and 10 men Rossy went down 4-0 to a strong Blackpool team. Rossendale did successfully defend the Rossendale Charity Cup overcoming Haslingden in the semi-final before thrashing Bacup 11-0 at Lanehead in the final, Lol Cook bagging a club record 6 goals. Off the field with gate receipts dropping by nearly a third the club was heading for a financial crisis if it could not make an immediate return to the top division.

1909-10

The club invested heavily to retain most of last season's squad although they did lose Harold Dawson who was signed by Everton for £110 and John Hall to Chorley, Arthur Evans was also sold to Blackpool, although the vastly experienced John Scott moved to Rossy as part of the deal. The club also brought in keeper James Fletcher from Carlisle and full back Amos Martincroft from Atherton and left half Ralph Bibby from Prescot.

The season opened with a 4-0 win over Oswaldtwistle Rovers and some fine football saw the club extend their unbeaten start to the season to seven games to lie in third place a but a run of three defeats including a 2-1 loss at leaders Glossop reserves saw the club slip to sixth. With John Scott deciding the journey to the valley was too much and signing for Fleetwood, Alf Berry moved into defence and inside forward Eddie Whiteside was brought in from Blackpool. The club bounced back with a four match unbeaten run including a 6-2 win in the first ever league clash with local rivals Bacup Borough. A 3-2 Boxing Day defeat at Haslingden saw our neighbours move above us into the last promotion place. A run of four wins saw the club rise to fifth, this run included a comfortable 4-0 win in the return game at Bacup and a 5-0 win over promotion rivals Stockport reserves where full back Martincroft scored 4 goals including a hat-trick of penalties, his fourth also coming from a penalty which the keeper saved and Martincroft scored from the rebound. This was followed by an embarrassing 10-1 reverse at Blackpool Reserves and a slump in form that meant only the last promotion place was attainable. A moral boosting 2-0 win over leaders Glossop reserves and a 3-0 win over close promotion rivals Haslingden lifted the team to fifth. The Haslingden game was played in front of a record crowd of around 5000, exact numbers are unknown as several hundred people rushed the gate as the game kicked off and entered the ground without paying, despite this the club reported record receipts of £96. A defeat at Eccles ended any hopes of promotion as the club finished sixth, eight points behind Rochdale in the last promotion place.

The FA Cup saw Padiham easily despatched 7-0 with Lol Cook scoring 5 goals, however a shock 3-1 home defeat to Walkden Central ended interest in the competition for another season. In the Lancashire Junior Cup Skelmersdale were beaten after a replay to set up a tie at Rochdale who proved too strong winning 4-0, whilst Bacup were beaten 5-4 as the club picked up the Rossendale Charity cup for a fourth time. On the player front Willie Ingham became the first player to score 100 goals for the club, whilst big Lol Cook broke the season goal scoring record with 45 goals in 42 games, 36 in the league.

However, off the field the club was in melt down as the high wage bill rumoured to be in the region of £15 a week had crippled the club and the wages had not been paid for several weeks leading to the players reporting the club to FA. With some gates as low as £12 during a harsh winter rumours were rife that the club would fold in the summer.

1910–11

The summer saw frantic activity to save the club, the whole of the playing squad had to be released due to unpaid wages after an FA investigation with club having to promise to pay outstanding debts to the players before other creditors. A series of fund raising events were held to save the club including a friendly against Oldham Athletic who had just won promotion to division one and enough money was raised to enable the club to start the season. The forced release of key players saw the club miss out on potential transfer fees as star players Ingham, Bibby and Whiteside were signed by former secretary Bert Stansfield who was now manager at Norwich City, Lol Cook moved to local rivals Bacup and Alf Berry was signed by Haslingden. With only amateur captain Raper Stott remaining from last season's team a host of new signings were brought in. Experienced centre half Tommy Matthews was brought in from Stockport County along with left half Harry Stott from St Helens whilst former Bradford Park Avenue winger Wilkie Ward was also signed. Most significantly Teddy Hill was enticed to sign, a talented inside forward who had given up the game after a short spell at Bury to concentrate on his business interests and cricket with Ramsbottom he was to give the club great service over the next few seasons.

The season opened with a five match unbeaten run including a 7-1 thrashing of Padiham which saw Hill mark his debut with a hat-trick. A 2-1 home defeat by Bacup in front of over 4000 fans helped boost the coffers but saw the club slip off the pace of the leading pack in a very competitive division. The club were boosted by the return to the club of former forward Jack Hall from Chorley to help take some of the goalscoring burden of the youthful Harry Hirst and Hill. A run of four wins from five games followed by a draw at league leader Hyde lifted the club up to fifth going into the Christmas period. Then a run of four wins and a draw saw the club go into the new year in third place. A run of inconsistent form saw the club slip off the pace to sixth and hopes of finishing in the top two disappeared at the beginning of April when the club lost to leading contenders Barrow, Chester and champions elect Haslingden although this game did bring in record receipts of £110. The season finished in remarkable fashion as the club broke its goalscoring record twice in a week defeating Ashton Town 14-0 at Dark Lane with young forward Dickie Day scoring 7 goals. The following Saturday, in the return fixture at Ashton Rossy won 17-0, Day this time bagging 6 goals, with Ritchie scoring 5 and Hirst 3. These results saw the club finish as the leagues leading scorers with a 126 goals for the season.

Not surprisingly given the turmoil at the start of the season there was little progress in the cups, Great Harwood were beaten 3-2 in the FA Cup before Colne won 1-0 in the next round. In the Lancashire Junior Cup Skelmersdale won 3-2 in the first round. The club did however retain the Rossendale Charity Cup beating Bacup 2-1 in the final at Dark Lane.

Off the field the season was a success as improved gates and fundraising efforts saw the club clear the debts owed to its former players as well as clear other debts. The club also received a massive boost at the league AGM where the resignation of the football league club reserve sides to join the Central League meant Rossy's seventh place finish in division two was enough to secure a place in the newly constituted top division of the Lancashire Combination.

1911-12

For the new season the club brought in William Cockerill as manager assisted by long serving trainer Johnny Weir whose service warranted a benefit match against Burnley. The club brought in wingers Tony Bond from Lancaster and Ed Berry from Leyland as well as much travelled Half back Percy Hartley from Rochdale

The season opened with just one win from the first five games and further moves were made to strengthen the team as keeper Jimmy Wyatt was brought in from Earlestown, Centre half Arthur Denny from Man Utd reserves and forward Tom Green from St Helens. There was some improvement in results but consistency remained elusive and a Christmas double over neighbours Accrington Stanley saw Rossy peak at seventh place. Even the return to the club of full back gentleman Jack Bardsley from Man City could not stop a run of seven games without a win before a strong finish to the season saw the club eventually finish eighth well behind Champions Rochdale.

There was more success in cup competitions in the FA Cup Portsmouth Rovers were thrashed 8-0 before Darwen were beaten 2-1 to set up a tie at Southport who proved too strong for a weakened Rossy team and ran out 4-1 winners. The Junior cup was to provide even more success Portsmouth Rovers were beaten 4-2 to set up a quarter final at Hindley Central who were well beaten 6-2 thanks to a hat-trick from Day. This set up a semi-final against local rivals Haslingden at Dark Lane a large crowd saw Rossy dominate for long periods and progress to the final thanks to first half goals from Berry and Hill. The final to be played at Rochdale saw Rossy up against Eccles Borough and in a tight game goals by Cornes and Hill were enough to see the club win the cup for the first time. The club also picked up the Rossendale Charity cup for the 4th year in succession after a 0-0 draw with Haslingden. Much to Haslingden's chagrin there was no provision for a replay and as holders Rossy retained the trophy.

The 1911–12 team with the Rossendale Charity Cup and Lancashire Junior Cup
Leading goal scorer Teddy Hill is 2nd from right on front row.

1912–13

If Rossendale were hoping to build on their Junior cup success, they were to be disappointed as cut backs meant half that side were tempted away from Dark Lane, Stott and Bardsley moving to Haslingden whilst Bond, Hartley, Slater and Gough also moved to greener pastures. The decision to move away from a team manager and revert back to a selection committee did not help and contributed to the terrible start to the season.

The season opened with a 5-1 defeat at home to Hyde and went downhill from there. Only three points were gained before the end of the year as the club slipped to the foot of the table and heavy defeats by Altrincham, Tranmere Rovers and a 10-0 defeat at Barrow meant the clubs position seemed hopeless. The club had lost start striker Day to Haslingden and Hill's appearances had been severely restricted by injury. So desperate were the club that they included England test cricketer Bill Hitch who was visiting his wife's family in Rawtenstall, at centre forward for the New Year's Day fixture with St Helens, he scored and his appearance boosted the attendance but the club still lost 2-1. The return of Hill from injury saw the club record their first win of the season when they beat fellow strugglers Denton 5-1 on the 1st of February. They followed this up with 3 wins from the next four games including a 4-1 demolition of title chasing Accrington Stanley at Dark Lane. Despite grabbing 20 points from their last 15 games the club had left themselves too much to do and finished in seventeenth place and were relegated back to division two.

There was little joy in the cups as a win over Padiham in the FA cup first qualifying round was followed by a heavy defeat at Southport in the next round. The defence of the Junior cup was ended at the first attempt with a 2-0 defeat at St Helens Rec and the clubs four year grip on the Rossendale Charity cup was ended after a semi-final defeat by Accrington Stanley.

1913–14

Rossendale kept the core of the side that was relegated the previous season and were boosted by the return of winger Tony Bond, they also signed youngster Harry Hastie from Padiham. Most importantly they retained the services of Teddy Hill who was a target for several big spending Southern League clubs, but he decided to stay due to his growing business interests in Ramsbottom.

The season opened with a 4-0 win over Denton but the club struggled for consistency losing four of the next six games. The return to the club of Raper Stott from Haslingden gave the club a timely boost that saw the team go on an eight match unbeaten run culminating in a 4-0 Boxing Day victory over Bacup at Dark Lane lifting them into the promotion places. They suffered a surprise defeat at Darwen the next day but bounced back with five wins from the next eight games to move into second place behind leaders Witton Albion. Promotion was secured on the 10th April with a 3-0 win over Stalybridge reserves thanks to Hill's third hat-trick of the season. A heavy 4-1 defeat at Witton the next day ended the club's championship ambitions and a return of one point from the last five game saw them finish in third place seven points behind champions Witton Albion.

The FA Cup saw Rossy overcome Breightmet Utd in the first qualifying round 4-2, but a Barnoldswick side containing several ex Rossy players proved too strong in the next round as Rossy went down 5-2.

In the Junior Cup Portsmouth Rovers were beaten 2-0 before the club were surprisingly beaten by Leyland after a replay in the second round.

The season was judged a success on the pitch, but it came at a cost as gates were disappointing and a loss of £52 was recorded for the season.

1914-15

The beginning of the season was overshadowed by the outbreak of the Great War but football continued largely unaffected, Rossy lost Raper Stott who had retired after twelve years great service to the club and winger Ed Berry moved to Glossop. With William Cockerill returning as team manager, Rossy brought in half back Ernie Bradshaw who had played a few games on loan from Burnley the previous season and former Burnley winger Arthur Beard.

The season opened with a fine 3-2 win at Nelson and three wins from the first four games saw the club in second place. The good form continued and by the beginning of December the club were in fourth place five points behind leaders Eccles. A run of four defeats started a slide down the table. A 4-0 win over title chasing Macclesfield stopped the rot but this was followed by five more defeats as the club slipped into the relegation places. By this time the war was starting to have an effect as several players such as Bradshaw left to join the army. As the country began to get on a war footing availability of players was affected with more local youngsters thrown into the team and results suffered accordingly. Wins over fellow strugglers Chorley and Northwich Victoria offered hope but defeats to Tranmere Rovers and Barrow condemned the club to fifteenth place one point off safety.

In the FA Cup Padiham were beaten 3-1 in the preliminary round but local rivals Haslingden knocked Rossy out in the next round after a replay. The Lancashire Junior Cup offered the club some respite from the league troubles as Haslingden were despatched 4-3 in the first round, the club needed a replay to dispose of Portsmouth Rovers in the quarter final to set up a semi-final against Leyland at Dark Lane where a Teddy Hill hat-trick set up a comfortable 5-1 win. This set up a final against Skelmersdale at Burnden Park and a large crowd saw a cracking game. Hastie fired Rossy into a first half lead Skelmersdale equalised on 51 minutes before taking the lead from the spot, Hampson equalised for Rossy on 82 minutes to set up extra time. Which Skelmersdale won with virtually the last kick off the match to break Rossy hearts.

At the end of the season normal football was suspended and the Lancashire Combination decided to run a scaled down regional competition.

The Rossendale team pictured before their home game with Nelson.

Back row: from left Cockerill(manager), Bradshaw, Shephard, Wyatt, Hastie, Hunter, Heyworth, Morris (trainer).

Front row: Taylor, Beard, Shuttleworth, Hill, Nuttall, Ryder.

1915–16

Rossendale decided to enter a team in the northern section of the Lancashire combination and using local players finished fourth in the league section which finished in January. The club then struggled in the subsidiary competition as it became increasingly difficult to field a team. With gates suffering as minds became increasingly focused on the terrible conflict in Europe the club decided to suspend activities until the end of the war at the end of the season.

The Inter War Years 1919–1939

1919-20

Football returned to Rossendale after World War One in September 1919 as Rossendale started their Lancashire Combination campaign with a squad of largely untried local amateurs, with only Tommy Heyworth and Jimmy Weir surviving from their last Lancashire combination campaign in 1916.

Rossy struggled initially losing their first three games including a 9-1 drubbing at Hurst, although Waterfoot youngsters Fred Smith and Harry Hall had impressed, the committee acted swiftly bringing in former players Billy Ingham who had returned north after several years at Norwich City and Tommy Kay along with new keeper Tony Smith from Openshaw. This led to an immediate improvement with four of the next five games being won. Consistency proved elusive however with good results such as Champions elect Chorley being defeated twice over Christmas being mixed with heavy defeats at the hands of Lancaster, Barrow and Eccles.

The only cup game saw Rossy lose to Accrington Stanley in the Lancashire Junior Cup in November. Further signings of the experienced Jimmy Wishart the former Halifax and Haslingden centre half and Harry Horner on the left wing continued to improve the squad. The final position of tenth was deemed a good return for the season.

Good support had meant the season was a success off the pitch with a surplus enabling Chairman Herbert Hoyle to announce that a £100 could be paid off outstanding debts and a further £35 being made available for ground improvements mainly to the old grandstand.

1920-21

The big news prior to the start of the 1920–21 season was the return of the legendary Billy Cook after his retirement from top class football with Oldham Athletic at the age of 38, the Rossy faithful would have to wait till the end of the cricket season to see their hero as he had a professional engagement with Lowerhouse in the Lancashire league.

Rossy once again started the season with three defeats, but the return of Cook saw a first win over Lancaster Town. The much awaited local derby with Bacup Borough in November saw a crowd of over 4000 at Dark Lane for a 1-1 draw, but it was Bacup who knocked Rossy out of the Lancashire junior Cup and won the inaugural Roscoe cup who shaded the bragging rights in the valley.

Once again Rossendale's league form was inconsistent as they finished a disappointing fourteenth. However, the form of teenager Wilf Chadwick who scored 14 goals in 15 games once he was switched from the wing to Centre forward was encouraging and attracting football league scouts to Dark Lane. At the end of the season left back Fred Smith was picked up by Bury where he enjoyed a ten year football league career much of it in the top flight.

Off the field the establishment of a Supporters club organisation helped improve the financial position and at the end of the season the lease on the ground was extended for a further ten years and the grandstand was purchased outright.

1921-22

In addition to losing Fred Smith to Bury, Billy Cook announced his retirement to concentrate on his cricket engagements and veteran Willie Ingham moved on. On the plus side full back Walter Taylor returned to his Newchurch roots for a second spell at the club, whilst winger Harry Horner also returned from Nelson, perhaps most significantly a young Mick Toman signed for the club after his release by Nelson.

The season started with a 3-0 win over Great Harwood thanks to a Wilf Chadwick hat-trick the first of five he was to score this season. Rossy found consistency hard to find until a run of four wins in November in which 19 goals were scored 11 of them by Chadwick shot them up the table. However, this was followed by a winless December. By now Wilf Chadwick's goalscoring exploits were attracting many league scouts to Dark Lane and he signed off with a hat trick at Rochdale Reserves in February, having scored 26 goals in 25 games before signing for Everton for £340. The season then petered out from this point as Rossy finished a disappointing tenth seventeen points behind Champions Lancaster Town. Despite the disappointing finish there were promising signs for the future with Wishart and Chapman starting to form an impressive partnership at half back, Harry Hall's versatility proving the players class and the progress of Toman and Jackie Kellett on the left wing giving fans hope for next season.

The Cup competitons offered little comfort for Rossy, in the FA Cup Cornholme who forfeited home advantage to benefit from a bigger gate were thrashed 6-1 thanks to another Chadwick hat-trick but had the consolation of a share of the 1700 gate, however, Darwen hammered Rossy 5-2 in the next round. Local rivals Bacup Borough ended Rossy's interest in the Lancashire Junior Cup in the first round and also won the Roscoe Cup. Off the field the supporters club donated another £187 to club funds which saw the covered accommodation on the popular side opposite the main stand completed.

This photo from 1922 has captain Jimmy Wishart seated at the centre, next to him 2nd from right is a young Mick Toman, Harry Hall is 4th from the left on the back row Wilf Chadwick is seated at the very front. Long serving trainer Johnny Weir is on the far right.

1922-23

The main signing prior to the start of this season was Irishman Paddy Quigley from Accrington Stanley, much was expected from the player who had played 13 games in the Third division north with Stanley and had Irish league experience with Glentoran. He did not disappoint scoring on his debut on the opening day as Rossy started with a comfortable 3-0 win over Hurst. Rossy won three of the first four games to threaten at the top of the table with early leaders New Brighton and Chorley. After a hiccup in form in the autumn the return of left winger Fred Kennedy to the club from Nelson gave the team a timely boost and with Jackie kellett switching to the right wing Rossy won the next five games scoring 23 goals as they moved into the top three and put themselves in contention for the title. Rossy entered April on the tail of leaders Chorley but a run of one point from four games including a vital 2-1 defeat at Chorley put an end to their ambitions and they had to be content with fifth place six points behind champions Chorley and the 85 goals scored made them the league's leading scorers.

Cup competitions offered little joy for Rossy with local rivals Bacup ending their interest in the inaugural Combination cup and Junior cup in the first round and also winning the Roscoe Cup. The FA cup saw Rossy overcome Leyland 7-4 before losing out to Fleetwood in a second replay after extra time. Overall Rossy had to be content with the progress made and the continued development of the team with Wishart and Chapman continuing to develop a good understanding in the half back line and Kellett and Toman providing quality going forward. Unfortunately, Rossy were to lose Paddy Quigley's whose 20 goals had earned him a second chance at Accrington and Fred Kennedy whose form on the wing had brought him to the attention of Manchester Utd.

1923-24

Rossendale started the season hoping to mount a challenge for the title, with youngster Len Crompton from Tottington establishing himself as first choice keeper, George Rushton coming in from Great Harwood at full back and the experienced Walker Hampson coming in at right half.

Rossy opened the season with four straight wins to top the table but then went ten league games without a win including five straight defeats on the run up to Christmas a run that had seen them slip into the bottom half of the table. This run had forced the club to bring in several new players, Peter Cowper a winger from Wigan Borough and centre forward John Williams from Bacup gave Rossy more of an attacking threat and five points out of six over Christmas stopped the rot. Unfortunately, a storm on the 8th January wrecked the main stand and the unforeseen cost this brought to the club brought on yet another financial crisis.

On the field a run of seven wins from the next nine games saw Rossy move back into the top five despite the loss of Mick Toman with injury for much of this period. The introduction of a young goalscoring inside forward in Albert Walmsley from Tottington saw the improved form extended to the end of the season and another fifth placed finish.

In the cup competitions Rossy beat Dick Kerrs in the FA Cup preliminary round only to lose to Morecambe in the next round, Morecambe also ended Rossy's interest in the combination cup.

The Junior cup offered Rossy hope as Burscough and Lancaster were disposed of in a run to the semi-finals but a disappointing performance saw Barnoldswick win the semi-final comfortably 4-0.

Rossy's fine second half of the season had once again seen football league scouts attracted to Dark Lane and they were to take advantage of Rossy's weak financial position caused by the cost incurred by the damage to the main stand to entice away some of Rossy's best young prospects, losing the services of Len Crompton to Blackpool, John Williams to Burnley, Peter Cowper to West Ham and Albert Walmsley to Middlesborough.

1924-25

Most of the pre-season activity was off the pitch with the storm damaged stand being rebuilt entirely with voluntary labour and financial support from the supporter's club. New signings included winger Frank Graham who had reserve experience at Blackburn Rovers and Crewe, forward Frank Gillibrand from Nelson and keeper Harry Lawson returning after a spell at league side Wigan Borough.

The season opened brightly with a 2-0 win over Atherton and Rossy were unbeaten in all competitions until the 27th September when they went down 2-1 to eventual champions Morecambe. A run of six wins in seven games up to the New Year saw Rossy in 3rd place and it could have been even better if the Eccles game which was abandoned with 10 minutes to go with Rossy winning 7-0 had not been ordered to be replayed.

Rossy struggled for consistency in the New Year and a run of one win in the last five games saw them eventually finish sixth. Rossendale did not enter the FA Cup due to the financial cost, so their cup interest was confined to the Lancashire Junior cup and the Combination Cup and in both cases rivals Chorley ended their interest in the competitions, although wins over Bacup, Leyland and Nelson had seen the club reach the Combination cup semi-finals for the first time before losing 4-0 at Chorley.

1925-26

Rossendale hopes of improving on last season's 6th place were boosted by the return to the club of Albert Walmsley from Middlesborough, whilst Crawshawbooth born Jimmy Dickenson returned to the valley after playing over 100 league games for Plymouth, the signing of full back Jack Kirkbright from Bacup completed Rossendale preparations, Rossendale were also to employ the services of a manager appointing Eli Nuttall from Bacup.

The season opened with a 4-0 win over Great Harwood and Rossendale remained in the top five for the first few months of the season. The Goalkeeping position was to be a problem though all season, Lawson was missing at the start of the season due to injury and when Duckworth the most likely replacement was injured in the 9-3 defeat by Lancaster, Lawson was forced to return earlier than expected and never produced the form of previous seasons. A run of five defeats to start the new year ended any hopes of making a serious challenge for the title and saw Rossy end an experiment with a manager. A strong finish saw them eventually finish third scoring a club record 119 goals, however they were 9 points adrift of eventual champions Nelson reserves.

Wins over Clitheroe and Darwen saw Rossy reach the semi finals of the Lancashire junior cup and like the previous season Chorley were to end Rossy's interest with a narrow 3-2 win at Victory Park. Nelson ended Rossy's interest in the Combination Cup when centre forward Pearson had to play in goal in a 6-2 defeat at home to Nelson reserves. Off the field the season was a success with the club reporting a profit on the season of over £346.

1926-27

Rossendale were optimistic of improving on the previous season 3rd place finish despite losing James Dickenson to Norwich City. The club were boosted by the return of the versatile Harry Hall from Bacup and the signing of half back Frank Walkden from Horwich RMI.

The season opened with a disappointing 1-0 reverse at Morecambe and when the club lost the services of experienced club captain Jimmy Wishart after a serious injury in the Roscoe cup defeat to Bacup things looked grim indeed. Rossy bounced back to win the next three games and the club extended this unbeaten run to eleven games to move into second place. Importantly during this run the club had solved the on-going goalkeeping problem by signing Percy Bury from Darwen, although the loss of centre forward Rodgers to Chorley threw up another problem. The good run ended with a disastrous 5-0 defeat at Horwich where supporter Alan Lord was drafted into the side to make up the numbers after two players were held up by a car crash. Rossy enjoyed a productive Christmas defeating Accrington Stanley Reserves 5-3 and Great Harwood 7-1 with new centre forward Fred Chilton scoring 5 goals however he was unable to agree terms with the club and left after a 3-1 defeat to Southport Reserves which saw Rossy slip to 3rd behind leaders Chorley and Morecambe. Young Benny Aspin was given a second chance at Centre forward for the next game with Hindley Green and scored in 7-1 win that set things up nicely for the visit of leaders Chorley on the 15th of January. A cracking game ended 4-4 but a 2-0 defeat in the return game at Victory Park the following week saw Rossy slip to fourth and hand their opponents the initiative in the title race. Rossy then reeled off four wins on the bounce including vital wins over Championship rivals Barnoldswick and Darwen but a shock 5-1 reverse at lowly Clitheroe saw them back in fourth place well adrift of the leading pack. Rossy then embarked on a remarkable run of victories that saw them chase down the leaders Chorley. On the 26th of April Rossy defeated bottom club Great Harwood 2-1 their eleventh consecutive win to top the table for the first time. Rossy completed their home fixtures by gaining revenge on Clitheroe with a 6-1 win with Benny Aspin grabbing a hat trick his 20th league goal in 20 games since securing the centre forward position in the New Year. The crowd of nearly 4000 for this game produced record gate receipts of £102 9s 6d. This win a record twelfth consecutive victory meant a point at Dick Kerr's on the last day of the season would secure Rossendale first Lancashire Combination Championship.

Saturday the 7th May saw 3000 Rossy fans make the journey to Preston for the Dick Kerr's game many on Special trains from Waterfoot station. Rossy started the game at Dick Kerr's nervously and found themselves 2-0 down inside the first 20 minutes but a goal by Toman settled the nerves and Harry Hall equalised before half time. The second half saw Rossy dominate play, but they failed to add to their tally and had to settle for the point that was enough to secure the title.

The celebrations went on well into the night with the players charabanc trip through Crawshawbooth, Rawtenstall and Waterfoot interrupted several times for speeches by captain Mick Toman to the crowds that lined the streets. The club showed a profit of£78 for the season the third season in a row the club had been in the black.

With the emphasis on the league not surprisingly Rossy did not achieve much success in cup competitions although wins over Wigan Borough Reserves and Great Harwood saw Rossy progress to the quarter finals of the Combination Cup before losing 5-1 at Morecambe, whilst in the Junior Cup Clitheroe were defeated before a 2-1 defeat at Lancaster ended Rossy's interest.

The Rossendale team and officials pictured with the 1926–27 Lancashire Combination trophy.

1927-28

Rossendale lost promising forwards Aspin and Haworth to Accrington Stanley, whilst Hogan moved on to Clitheroe, Stanley Greenhalgh from Barnoldswick, Jack Hall a former Man Utd reserve and Fearnley a Burnley reserve were brought in to replace them, but none of them proved up to the task as Rossy made a difficult start to the season winning only two of their first nine league games.

Rossy acted swiftly to rectify their failings bringing back Centre forward John Williams to the club after his release by Burnley and signing Harry Hurst an inside forward from Lancaster. Result improved especially in cup competitions with Williams scoring freely, but league form was inconsistent. Off the field disaster struck at the end of October when the uninsured stand roof was blown off during a ferocious storm. November ended with a 3-1 defeat at leaders Chorley leaving Rossy in tenth place. The club was having more success in both the Combination and Lancashire junior Cups and this meant Rossy had plenty of games in hand on the leaders. January saw Rossy start a thirteen game unbeaten run including a 5-2 win over leaders Chorley moving them into the top four and giving Rossy hope they could defend their title. However a run of one win in their last five games meant Rossy had to content themselves with fifth place ten points adrift of champions Chorley.

It was in the cup competitions that Rossy enjoyed most success. In the Junior Cup Fleetwood, Burscough and Horwich were disposed of to set up a final against Lancaster at Ewood Park on the 28th January. A crowd of 7,700 saw a closely contested game which Rossy looked like winning for long periods, hitting the woodwork three times before Lancaster snatched victory with a Marquis goal 7 minutes from time. Rossy sought consolation in the Combination Cup defeating Accrington Stanley reserves, Barnoldswick, Nelson Reserves and Burscough to set up a final with Horwich RM. Horwich won the toss for venue and this proved decisive as Rossy struggled with the notorious Grundy Hill slope in a game dominated by the hosts for long periods. However, it took a disputed penalty converted by Keetley for the hosts to break the deadlock, Keetley added a second late in the game to confirm victory for Horwich. Rossy gained some consolation winning the East Lancs Charity Cup defeating Darwen 2-1 after extra time thanks to a stunning strike from Williams the penultimate goal of a club record 53 in a season for the centre forward.

1928-29

The opening day of the season saw the club unveil their rebuilt main stand, now with 750 seats and a tea hut built at a cost of £1000, it was opened by league president TP Campbell who claimed this made Rossendale's Dark Lane ground on of the best in the League. Rossendale had three new signings for the start of the season all with football league experience, centre half Alf Kellett from Rochdale, brother of left winger Jack Kellett, George Spence a right winger from Nelson and Harry Hird an inside forward with experience at Bury, Blackpool and New Brighton. Unfortunately, only Hird was to prove a success as Rossy made a slow start with only one win in their first five games.

The return of Toman from injury and Williams starting to repeat the goalscoring form of the previous season with 14 goals in eight games saw Rossy move up the table. A run of ten wins in eleven games into the New Year saw Rossy move into second place behind leaders Chorley. A run of one point from three games at the beginning of April ended Rossy's championship dreams, but Rossy still had hopes of runners up spot going into the last game of the season, however despite winning 5-0 at Manchester Central they missed out to Horwich RMI by 1/25th of a goal, on goal average.

Rossy made an early exit from the Junior cup at the hands of Morecambe, but enjoyed a successful run in the Combination Cup defeating Accrington Stanley Reserves and Bacup, before beating Lancaster 2-0 in the semi-final at Dark Lane in front of 3500 fans.

Rossendale won the toss this year and hosted the final against Southport reserves. Rossy dominated the first half and goals by Williams and Hird gave the host a 2-0 advantage at half time. Rossendale missed several chances to increase the lead before Mundy pulled a goal back for Southport on 70 minutes, but Rossy held on to win the Combination cup for the first time in the club's history in front of nearly 3000 fans who paid over £80. Centre forward John Williams finished the season with 56 goals in 40 games beating the club record he set the previous season.

The Rossendale team and officials with the Lancashire Combination cup Percy Bury is centre of the middle row with Harry Hall 3rd from right. Jack Kirkbright is 2nd from left then Frank Walkden, with captain Mick Toman to the right of the impressive trophy, then John Williams.

1929-30

Rossendale made only one major signing before the season picking up winger Arthur Bromilow from Atherton. Once again Rossy made a slow start winning only one of their first six games. They were then rocked when leading scorer Williams announced he would be giving up the game due to his work commitments.

Rossy made light of this set back and inspired by classy inside forwards Hird and Toman embarked on a ten match unbeaten run that lifted them up to 6th. The committee acted swiftly to the loss of Williams by bringing in experienced forward George Yates from Darwen who had league experience with Wigan Borough along with right back Fred Blinkhorn from Burnley. Inconsistent form in March and April saw the club slip back down the table before three wins in the last four games saw the club recover to finish eighth.

The fact that Rossy used 35 players showed the club was now going through a transitional phase after the success of the recent seasons. Cup competitions brought little joy going out of all competitions at the first hurdle including an embarrassing 9-0 defeat at Chorley in a Junior Cup replay.

1930-31

With keeper Percy Bury moving on, Mick Toman was now the sole survivor from the Championship winning team of four seasons ago. Rossy also lost Harry Hird who announced his retirement, but brought in Arthur Town a goalkeeper who had been playing in Burnley's A team, Jim Tomlinson a halfback from Morecambe who had league experience with Accrington Stanley and inside forward Jimmy Gee from Clitheroe who also had league experience with Stanley.

After losing the first two games Rossy improved winning six of the next nine games to move up to 7th. The centre forward position was proving a problem with Yates injured and Rossy resorted to tempting Harry Hargreaves out of the retirement and the former Burnley, Spurs and Wolves forward responded with six goals in eight games before he broke down injured. This was typical of an inconsistant season that saw much chopping and changing, with money being spent bringing experienced players such as Tommy Mandy the ex Southport and Wigan Borough winger with little success as Rossy finished fifteenth their lowest finish since football resumed after World War One.

Cup competitions once again offered little joy although Rossy progressed past the first hurdle in both the junior and combination cups beating Lytham and Bacup respectively before losing to Lancaster and Nelson in the second round.

1931-32

Three key signings were made before the start of the season goalkeeper Sam Collier was picked up from Wigan Borough, full back Tom Partington from Oldham athletic and forward Joe Myerscough who had league experience with Man Utd and Bradford PA was signed from Lancaster.

The season started brightly with an unbeaten four match run. However, three heavy defeats followed and the committee acted swiftly bringing back half back Ralph Haworth from Accrington Stanley, left back Ben Brelsford from Manchester North End, right winger Dowden from Colne and experienced left winger Tommy Moon from Burscough.

Results did improve but consistency was hard to find with a 9-0 thrashing of Accrington Stanley reserves followed by three defeats. Rossy saw in the new year in 12th position. The return to the club of Joe Lyons who had played a key role in winning the championship five seasons ago stiffened the defence and the introduction of local youngster Boocock up front added some pace to the forward line as the club gradually climbed up the table to finish a creditable sixth 11 points behind champions Darwen.

Once again Rossy lost in the first round of the Combination cup at Great Harwood, but made progress in the Junior Cup beating Bacup and Hindsford to reach the quarter finals where they surprisingly lost heavily at home to Dick Kerr's.

Off the field the end of the season was overshadowed by a financial crisis as the new stand pushed up the rateable value of the ground and the governments increase in the entertainment tax forced up gate prices and saw a drop in attendances. This led to an exodus of players at the end of the season with only three professionals Jimmy Gee, Mick Toman and Tom Partington offered terms. The committee also decided to bring in a team manager for next season in Joe Campbell who had football league experience with Rochdale and Wigan Boro and had recently been manager of Great Harwood.

1932-33

The new season saw an influx of new players many with football league experience such as, veteran William Stage the former Bury and Burnley player and Billy Tompkinson the ex stockport winger.

Despite a reasonable start with four wins from the first seven games the new players by and large failed to deliver and the high turnover of players saw the club win just once in the next seventeen league games. This run cost manager Campbell his job, the committee taking charge of team affairs with the help of trainer Charlie Morris. There was no immediate improvement in results, but the harsh winter meant there was a backlog of fixtures and Rossy gained some momentum during this busy run of games losing just three of the last twelve to pull away from the bottom of the table to finish fifteenth.

Once again, the cup competitions offered little respite, losing heavily to Darwen in the first round of the Junior cup and making second round exits in the Combination cup and East Lancs Charity cup. Although they did beat Bacup 5-4 over two legs in the revived Rossendale Charity Cup at the end of the season. Off the field the committee made arrangements for the club to buy the ground from owner H Bolton JP, this combined with the poor season led to a loss of £380 for the year.

1933-34

Eli Nuttall was placed in charge of team affairs for the start of the season and he brought in three players from neighbours Accrington Stanley, Winger George Dewsnap, experienced left Back Tom Whittaker who was made club captain and half back Ralph Haworth who returned to Rossy for a third spell. Former Welsh international Centre Half Billy Matthews was also signed from Colwyn Bay.

The season started fairly brightly with four wins from the first six league games that saw Rossy in eighth position, but the worsening financial position at the club meant it was increasingly difficult to retain a settled team and a run of five league defeats and first round defeats in the FA Cup and Combination Cup saw Eli Nuttall removed from his position at the end of October.

Club stalwart Mick Toman was placed in charge of team affairs and there was a temporary improvement in results, but the Christmas period and early new year saw an horrendous run of results culminating in a 9-1 thrashing by Clitheroe at Dark Lane. Toman acted swiftly bringing in Right back Harry Stansfield who had league experience with Swindon, former Rossy keeper Len Crompton from Norwich City, Blackpool legend Billy Benton and prolific striker John Jepson from Nelson. This helped stop the rot on the field but the financial crisis off the field saw top scorer, Centre forward Syd Johnson allowed to leave and a crisis meeting was held in February to discuss ways of resolving the clubs worrying £300 debt. It was decided a share issue would take place to resolve the problem however of the £500 worth of shares issued only £99 was taken up. Against this background Toman managed to restore stability despite using 52 players over the course of the season to secure a 14th place finish.

The FA Cup was entered for the first time in 10 years but brought no joy as Rossy bowed out at the first attempt to lowly Westhoughton. There were first round exits in the Combination cup at the hands of Bacup and in the Junior Cup at the hands of Lancaster Town. Bacup also defeated Rossy over two legs in the end of season Rossendale Challenge Cup. Despite the cost cutting measures the Chairman W Gregson announced a loss of £182 for the season.

1934-35

Manager Toman was busy in preseason bringing in several new signings, G Vickers the former Darwen goalkeeper was signed, Hulbert Barnes a half back from Bacup, winger Andy Mitchell was signed from Northampton Town along with former Leeds Utd inside forward Billy Bennett from Southport. Centre forward Frank Ainsworth was snapped up from Nelson and Tommy Aspin from Barnoldswick.

With the experienced Stansfield, Whittaker, Benton and Grimshaw joining the new signings in defence and local lad Dick Haworth given the left wing birth the new season started well with four wins in the first five games, new forward Ainsworth bagging eight goals in those games. Rossy made an early exit at the hands of Skelmersdale in the FA Cup and suffered their first league defeat at Clitheroe at the end of September. They then went on a run of eight consecutive league victories to move up to fourth. Left winger Haworth was signed by Oldham Athletic, but Toman acted swiftly to pick up Tom Badger from Lancaster as a replacement. The good results and success seen against league clubs in the Lancashire senior cup had seen the crowds flood back to Dark Lane and the Christmas day win over Fleetwood was watched by over 3000. The last game of the year saw second placed Rossy travel to leaders Lancaster and a keenly fought contest was anticipated. Unfortunately Rossy who played much of the game with 10 men after an injury to Bennett were totally outplayed and lost 10-0. Rossy did bounce back immediately giving 15 year old Tommy Lawton his debut the following week against Leyland Motors and he obliged with an hat-trick in a 9-0 win before joining Burnley. Rossy struggled to produce the outstanding form of the first part of the season but entered April in fourth place and still in contention for the title. However, Billy Bennett broke his leg in a 4-0 defeat at Nelson and Rossy never recovered as the season petered out and Rossy had to be content with fifth place 10 points behind Champions Lancaster.

The Cup competitions offered Rossy some joy for a change, after an early exit from the FA Cup Rossy reached the Quarter finals of the Lancashire Junior Cup before losing at Wigan Athletic, they also enjoyed a good run in the Combination cup beating Bacup, Rochdale res and Nelson before suffering a shock 4-1 defeat Clitheroe in the semi-final.

However, it was the entry into the Lancashire Senior Cup of non-league teams for the first time since before the First world War that really caught the imagination and Rossy did not disappoint. In the first round Rossy were held at home by Burnley but won the replay 1-0. This set up a plumb tie against Man Utd at Old Trafford and over a 1000 Rossy supporters made the journey on two specially chartered trains to witness a fantastic 2-1 win. This set up a quarter final tie with Liverpool at Dark Lane and a crowd of 3412 saw Rossy lose narrowly 2-1 to a team containing 8 players with football league experience. These games generated gate receipts totalling nearly £400 of which Rossy would take 40% and this coupled with fund raising events that raised £900 went a long way to securing Rossy's financial future. The club were shocked when Manager Toman announced his resignation due to work commitments, but everybody at the club was delighted when he was persuaded to change his mind.

1935-36

In the close season Rossy lost Billy Benton who retired and Centre forward Frank Ainsworth who returned to Nelson. They were replaced by the experienced Archie Jackson from Manchester North End and the much travelled forward Tommy Wyper from Crewe. Other signings included winger Harry Spink from Oldham and Harry Chadwick from Stalybridge.

Once again, the season started brightly with a 3-0 win over Darwen and a 7-1 win at Bacup in the first few games. A run of five defeats in October saw Rossy slip to fifteenth in the table. There were occasional good results such as wins over title chasing South Liverpool and Chorley, but the high turnover in players meant consistency was difficult to achieve as forty four players were used over the course of the season. The one highlight was the emergence of 19 year old forward Cyril Crawshaw who bagged 17 goals in 22 games. The season ended disastrously with only two points from the last ten games as Rossy finished nineteenth. Manager Toman had to give many local youngsters a chance as once again the financial situation worsened.

Again, it was the Lancashire Senior Cup that proved the highlight of Rossy's season as top flight sides Bolton and Preston were beaten before eventual winners Blackpool defeated Rossy 3-1 before a Dark Lane crowd of 3959. Rossy proved less successful in other cup competitions making first round exits in the FA Cup at Great Harwood and the East Lancs Charity cup at Accrington Stanley reserves. The club did reach the second rounds of the Junior cup and Combination cup, before defeats at Wigan Athletic and Nelson respectively.

The season ended with a stormy AGM with chairman Bert McLay coming under pressure for paying high wages for elderly professionals at the end of their careers instead of trying to discover more young players like Crawshaw, which resulted in a massive loss of £403 for the season.

Rossendale team from 1935–36 part of the Ardath Tobacco company cigarette card collection.

Back row: from left to right H. Barnes, A. Jackson, G. Vickers, A. Pickering, H. Chadwickand C. Morris trainer.

Front row: E. Hall, J. Calvert, H. Wyper, H. Stansfield Capt, T. Whittaker and H. Spink.

1936-37

Once again manager Toman brought in an influx of new players half back Harry Hurst and forward Albert Wright were brought in from Chorley, whilst inside forward Fank Eaton and full back Norris Rawlinson were signed from Macclesfield and centre half Norman Crompton from Lancaster. Also left winger Dick Howarth returned to the club after a spell at Oldham Athletic.

The season opened with a record opening day victory for the club 7-2 at Great Harwood. The club also won their first FA cup tie since returning to the competition four seasons ago. September ended with the club in eighth position. However, the team's weakness in defence was highlighted by twice conceding 7 goals at Chorley and Lancaster. Manager Toman's attempt to rectify these problems were increasingly frustrated by the club's financial position and this came to a head in December when young forward Cyril Crawshaw was sold to Rochdale and Toman could not agree with the board how to readjust the wage bill and resigned ending a fifteen year association with the club.

The committee then took charge of team selection with disastrous results as only two games were won out of the next twenty two with several horrendous defeats with 10 goals being conceded at New Brighton reserves and 9 at Barrow reserves. Eventually the club appointed Reuben Butler as manager in March and with the club boosted by a run in the Combination cup managed to win their last three games to finish nineteenth and avoid re-election.

In the cup competitions after defeating Lytham in the FA cup they lost to Horwich in the next round and went out at the first attempt in the Junior Cup and East Lancs Charity Cup. In the Combination cup the club enjoyed some success beating Clitheroe before drawing at Chorley in November, the harsh winter meant the replay was not until early April and a Rossy win set up a semi-final clash at neighbours Bacup which Rossy won 1-0 to set up a final against Barrow Reserves. The league mysteriously decided the tie should be played at South Liverpool on a Tuesday evening, not surprisingly the game was poorly attended as both sets of supporters struggled to get to the game which a strong Barrow team won 3-1.

The turmoil at the club in the New Year led to an EGM and the election of a new board with Dr Purcell as Chairman, charged with getting the club back on an even keel as losses for the season stood at over £400 for the second season in a row.

1937-38

Manager Reuben Butler rocked Rossy when he moved to Great Harwood in the summer and he was replaced by Mr L Cardwell. New signings included full back Leigh from Accrington Stanley, inside forward Flanagan from Burnley reserves and left winger Alder from Buxton.

The team made their best ever start to a season winning the first five games to top the league and with crowds around the 2000 mark, things were looking good as Rossendale strengthened their squad with the signing of experienced local man Jack Schofield from Accrington Stanley. However, the first sign that all was not well came at the end of September when Chairman Dr Purcell resigned, this was closely followed by the clubs exit from the FA cup when the club threw away a two goal lead at Chorley. The club then went on a seven match run without a win during which Flanagan, right winger Lythgoe and leading scorer Albert Wright all left as the club slipped to mid table. The goalscoring exploits of youngster Jack Isherwood who bagged 32 goals in his first full season ensured the club slipped no lower and the club were content with a ninth place finish two point clear of local rivals Bacup.

The cups did not overflow for Rossy as they went out of the FA Cup in the second qualifying round, were hammered 5-0 at South Liverpool in the Junior Cup and lost to rivals Bacup in the second round of the combination cup.

1938–39

During the close season the club improved the drainage on the pitch and the stand roof was extended to provide cover for the enclosure. The first game saw the unveiling of a new electronic clock on the stand roof. New signings included full backs Idris Williams from Rochdale and Harold Readett from Hurst and forward Herbert Fox from Manchester North End.

The season started well with six wins from the first eight league games that saw Rossy in second place one point behind leaders Accrington Stanley Reserves at the beginning of October. The club extended their unbeaten run to thirteen games before a surprise defeat at home to local rivals Bacup at the end of November. Further defeats followed against title rivals South Liverpool and Bangor City, but the club ended the Christmas period in third place two points behind leaders South Liverpool. An injury to Readett highlighted Rossendale's defensive deficiencies, only one more clean sheet was kept as their Championship challenge fizzled out with a glut of goals at both ends. Rossy eventually finished sixth 12 points behind Champions South Liverpool with 110 goals for and 95 goals against. Once again young Jack Isherwood was the pick of the forwards with 33 league goals.

Cup competitions were once agains disappointing with first round exits in the FA Cup, Combination Cup and East Lancs Charity Cup. The club beat Morecambe in the Junior Cup to earn a tie with Wigan Athletic in the quarter-finals but were well beaten 3-1 in front of a large crowd at Dark lane.

World War II 1939-45

The 1938–39 season started with a record 9 0 victory over Horwich RMI, with all five forwards getting on the scoresheet, this was followed by a creditable 3-3 draw at fancied Chorley but Hitler invaded Poland and the season was suspended.

After a month of the so called phoney war the Lancashire Combination decided to start a war time competition and eleven teams entered, including Rossendale who eventually finishing third behind Chorley. The Combination Cup and Junior Cup competitions were also run and Rossy reached the semi-finals of both competitions losing to eventual winners Chorley and Rochdale Reserves respectively.

The Lancashire FA decided it could not sanction any competitions the following season, so Rossendale entered the Manchester League and enjoyed a successful season missing out on winning the league after a last day defeat to Newton Heath Locos. The withdrawal from the league of Manchester Utd reserves and Denton cost the club ten points and a league competition they had led for most of the season.

The club had the consolation of winning the league cup the Gylgryst Cup defeating Hyde Utd 5-4 in the final. Bacup were beaten 8-0 in the first round and the semi-final was notable as Rossendale defeated Droylesden 15-4 with Jack Isherwood scoring a club record nine goals in the game.

The Rossendale team and officials pictured with the Gilgryst Cup they won in 1941.

1941–42 saw the return of the Lancashire Combination which ran a 10 team league which was dominated by the Blackpool services team an army team made up of professional footballers, Rossendale did well to finish fourth as the league also included four football league reserve sides. The Combination cup was played on a mini league basis and Rossendale did well battling their way to the final against Blackpool services that attracted a record crowd of nearly 6000 and receipts of £97 to Dark Lane for the final. Unfortunately, the Blackpool team was too strong and ran out easy 5-1 victors.

Rossendale also enjoyed a good cup run in the Junior cup reaching the semi final before losing 7-5 on aggregate to Chorley in the two legged tie. Financially the large gates attracted by the professional sides proved beneficial to Rossendale who cleared a debt of £495 during the season.

The 1942–43 season saw only six teams enter the Lancashire Combination which was once again won by Blackpool Services with Rossendale finishing third. Rossendale reached the semi-finals of the junior Cup losing to eventual winners Blackpool services 10-3 0ver two legs. The Combination cup was played on a league basis with the top four going into the semi-finals, Rossy once again fought their way into a two legged final this time against Chorley. Rossendale won the first leg 2-0 in front of a healthy crowd but lost the return leg 3-0 to lose the tie.

The 1943-44 season once again saw a seven team league but with the war beginning to make a big impact, only Rossendale, Chorley and a weakened Blackpool services team remained, the rest of the league was made up of works teams such as De Haviland and Howard & Bulloughs. With much of the Rossendale valley industry turned over to war work and many workers therefore in protected trades Rossendale had a generous pool of players to select from and with a healthy financial position the club was able to keep a strong team together. This helped Rossendale achieve a league and combination cup double. The club won nine of their twelve league games to comfortably win the Lancashire Combination and Howard & Bulloughs were beaten 4-1 on aggregate in the two legged Combination Cup final. The club also reached the Junior Cup final drawing the first leg with Blackpool Services 1-1 at Dark Lane before losing the second leg 4-2 at Bloomfield Road.

With the war reaching a climax there was no senior non league football during the 1944-45 season although the club did enter an amateur team in the Burnley and District war time league.

1945-46

Lancashire Combination football returned in September 1945 with a twelve team league and Rossendale started well winning four of their first six games including a 5-3 win at favourites Chorley. However, this form soon attracted football league scouts to Dark Lane and goalkeeper Walker Grimsditch was snapped up by Southport and centre forward Joe Hargreaves was signed by Rochdale. Despite these setbacks Rossendale remained in contention until a run of one win from their final six league games saw them slip to 6th 10 points behind Champions Chorley.

The second half of the season was taken up with the Combination cup which was once again run on a league basis and with the club boosted by the return of prolific forward Jack Isherwood from the army Rossy battled their way through to the semi finals, where they were drawn away to local rivals Bacup Borough. The Bacup side containing several ex Rossy players won 3-0 to prevent Rossy defending the trophy they had held since 1944.

Rossendale enjoyed more cup success in the Junior cup defeating Leyland Motors, Barrow reserves and South Liverpool to set up a final against Chorley at Burnden Park Bolton. A crowd of 4792 saw Rossy dominate much of the game to lead 2-0 midway through the second half. Chorley fought back and equalised in the 88th minute to set up a reply at Turf Moor. The replay saw Rossy once again take the lead early in the first half but Chorley equalised immediately and the tie was settled by two goals in a minute by Chorley early in the second half, Rossy pulled a goal back late in the game but Chorley broke away to score a fourth and secured a 4-2 win in front of over 6000 fans.

The Post-War Years

1946-47

The Lancashire Combination returned to its full quota of 22 clubs and Rossy saw pre-war players Billy Palmer. Jack Isherwood and Alder return to the club, they were joined by Cyril Crawshaw early in the season and with new signings James Martin and John Shadwell adding league experience the club started the season with a five match unbeaten run to challenge at the top.

A run of three defeats in October saw the club slip off the pace and with the prolific Martin suffering a career ending injury and Isherwood joining several ex Rossy players at Champions elect Bacup early in the new year the club dropped steadily down the league to finish 20th narrowly avoiding relegation to the newly formed second division.

The particularly harsh winter which saw just four league games played in over two months between January and April meant the season was extended until the 14th of June. Cup games offered little relief to Rossy who went out in the second round of the Junior Cup at South Liverpool and lost to Bacup after two replays in the Combination Cup.

1947-48

The new season saw several new signings, Goalkeeper Walker Grimsditch returned to the club after spells at Southport, full back Ellis Cornwell was signed from Accrington Stanley, George Haigh a former Burnley reserve with league experience at Stockport filled the centre half birth and Scots winger Alex Carruthers was signed from Rochdale.

The season started with a 6-2 win over Southport reserves but the team lacked consistency and never really ventured above mid table drawing 12 games more than any other team in the league, before eventually finishing fifteenth.

Over 40 players were used and several key players established themselves in the team including Johnny Clark, Bill Craig and Norman Berry. The club saw cup success in the Combination Cup beating Rochdale reserves, Great Harwood and Horwich to set up a semi-final against Prescot that went to two replays generating £470 in gate receipts before Prescot won through 2-0 at Dark Lane. The Lancashire junior Cup saw Rossy drop to a shock defeat at home to Astley Bridge.

Off the field gate receipts were generally disappointing although the last game of the season saw receipts of £74 the best of the season as Wigan clinched the Combination title with a 3-1 victory. Despite this Chairman Norman Broadley announced that major work levelling and re-turfing the pitch was to take place over the close season.

1948-49

With £1700 spent on levelling the playing surface and several new signings, including goalkeeper Harry Atherton from Burnley, Frank Ashworth from Netherfield and Tommy Nuttall from Bacup, Rossy were hopeful of enjoying a successful season. The club were also boosted when Norman Berry turned down Leeds Utd offer to turn professional to remain at Dark Lane.

Early season hopes were dashed as three of the first four games were lost, although a run of three wins saw the club rise to ninth by the end of September. The club also embarked on a record breaking FA Cup run and with Alf Davies finally establishing himself at Centre forward after the departure of Jack Bannister the goals began to flow. Although the cup run did prove a distraction as league results were inconsistent. Netherfield finally ended the FA Cup run in the 4th qualifying round in November, Rossendale best ever run in the FA cup at that time.

After a boxing day win over local rivals Bacup the club lost five of the next six games to slip down the league table but boosted once again by a good run in the Combination cup Rossendale put together a run of just one defeat in twelve league games to ensure a comfortable mid table finish.

The club also beat Belle Vue , Bacup, Fleetwood and Lytham to reach the final of the Combination cup. The club met Bangor City in the final at Springfield Park Wigan. Rossendale dominated the first half forcing Bangor keeper Vance to make several fine saves and thought they had taken the lead on 33 minutes when Davies appeared to bundle the ball home only for the referee to pull play back for hand ball and award Rossy a penalty. Captain George Haigh stepped up to take the kick but blazed the ball over the bar. Boosted by this Bangor gradually fought their way back into the game but neither side could break the deadlock forcing the game into extra time. Bangor looked the stronger team in the extra period and it was no surprise when Longden fired home the all-important goal on 110 minutes to consign Rossy to runners up.

Overall, the season was deemed a successful one with gate receipts boosted by the two good cup runs and the discovery of prolific centre forward Alf Davies who bagged 44 goals in all competitions.

1949-50

With most of last season's side retained the main new signing was winger Fred Greenhalgh from Droylesden and with optimism high the season started in fine style with five consecutive league wins to top the league, striker Alf Davies netting in each one and with the club embarking on another good run in the FA cup things were looking bright.

However, the news that star striker Davies was emigrating to Canada seemed to knock the stuffing out of the team and they had to wait till Christmas eve for their next league victory. The club progressed to the 3rd qualifying round of the FA Cup before a 5-0 defeat at Fleetwood in Davies's penultimate game ended their interest for another year. A mini revival over Christmas and the new year ensured mid table security but the club struggled to replace Davies and even tried left back Johnny Clark at centre forward, they were also hampered by the loss of Norman Berry for several games due to his selection for county and north of England amateur representative sides.

The Combination cup and Junior Cup also offered little joy in a disappointing season that saw average gate receipts drop to £51 and financial difficulties once again appear on the horizon.

1950-51

To cut costs the club decided to retain just five professionals from the previous season plus leading amateur Norman Berry, with one of the professionals keeper Harry Atherton missing the first six weeks of the season due to an operation, the club were relying on local amateurs to step up to the mark. This hope was seriously misplaced as the club made a disastrous start to the season picking up just one point from the first ten league games the clubs worst ever start to a season. In fact, the first sixteen games in all competitions brought just a solitary FA Cup win over Horwich.

With the club rooted to the foot of the table going into October new Chairman Billy Holden acted Swiftly to stop the rot bringing in several new professionals in Mann, Don Strachan from Fleetwood and most importantly former Man City centre half Eric Eastwood and future England international Eddie Clamp who was unable to play professional football due to a dual registration dispute between Burnley and Wolves. With keeper Atherton also returning these signings had an instant impact as the club then won their first league game against Darwen on the 21st October. The club then extended the run to seven consecutive wins to move out of the relegation zone. The harsh winter weather the disrupted the run and just of one point from seven games in April saw the club slip dangerously close to the relegation zone again. A 2-1 win at home to Clitheroe on the 2nd of May finally secured safety for the club.

Not surprisingly the club enjoyed little cup success although they did beat Champions elect wigan Athletic to reach the quarter finals of the Junior Cup before losing to Morecambe. Off the field the financial difficulties the club faced led to an offer from Rossendale council to move to Newhallhey, but at an EGM the club decided to remain at Dark Lane.

1951-52

The club made several new signings hoping to avoid the tribulations of the previous season, the main signing being winger Tommy Henderson after his release by Burnley and half back Ben Crossland from Nelson.

The season opened with a 4-1 over Bootle Athletic, but wins proved elusive with only two more recorded before November leaving the club mired in a relegation battle at the foot of the table. The club brought in forwards Jim Farrington from Stalybridge and Don Francis from Clitheroe and a three match unbeaten run in November the best of the season bought the club some breathing space over relegation rivals St Helens, Earlestown and Darwen. A run of only one win from the next 10 games saw Rossy slip back into trouble, a vital 4-3 win over bottom club Earlestown at the end of March kept the club out of the bottom two, but safety was not guaranteed until a surprise 3-2 win at 4th placed Wigan Athletic in the penultimate game of the season.

Cup competitions brought little joy with only two wins recorded one in the FA Cup and one in the Junior Cup. Off the field the poor form saw a collapse in gate receipts and led to the club losing £473 over the season despite a contribution of £333 from the Supporters club.

1952-53

Rossendale invested quite heavily in new players to avoid another relegation battle bringing in former Rochdale full back Jack Dougall from Nelson, former Burnley player Gordon Haigh from Watford, Ronnie Wood also returned after a year on Bury's books, whilst promising young keeper Geoff Smith was also signed from Nelson.

The season started promisingly with three wins out of the first four league games, but the club struggled go put a good run of results together and slipped down to mid table. The club were boosted financially when Bradford City stepped in to sign young keeper Geoff Smith after some impressive performances. The clubs form was consistently inconsistent as they remained stuck in mid table all season producing good results against top teams such as a 4-0 win over Darwen and 5-0 win over Marine but these results were mixed with 8-0 thrashing at Wigan Athletic and 6-2 at home to Horwich.

The club eventually finished 14th but gates remained disappointing and the club recorded a loss for the fifth successive season, this despite a half crown appeal that raised £628 for the club. Chairman Billy Holden appealed for more support from the valley claiming the club needed average gates of £90 per game to compete with their closest rivals in the Lancashire Combination.

Once again there was no cup runs to enjoy as the only success was an FA cup win over Darwen as the club fell at the first hurdle in all the other competitions.

1953-54

Rossendale's main signing was experienced goalkeeper Mark Radcliffe from Rochdale in an attempt to solve a goalkeeping problem that had existed since the departure of Smith the previous season, this problem persisted during a difficult season as the club used seven different keepers during the season.

The season opened with a win over Horwich, but they had to wait nine games for their next league win and by November the club were bottom of the league, although the open nature of the league meant they were only four points behind the sixth placed club. The club brought in experienced inside forward Walter Keeley from Fleetwood to add some guile to the forward line but results remained inconsistent and a run of one win in eight games in the new year had alarm bells ringing.

The club brought in mercurial scots forward Willie Brown from Nelson with immediate effect as four of the next five games were won lifting the club off the bottom of the table. The Easter period proved crucial to Rossy's survival as it brought a shock 5-0 win over champions elect Wigan Athletic and a vital 3-0 win over relegation rivals Chorley. Safety was secured in the penultimate game with a 2-2 draw at South Liverpool, the club eventually finishing 13th three points clear of relegation in a remarkable season that saw relegated Prescot finish just six points behind seventh placed South Liverpool.

Once again, the cup competitions offered little respite with the only highlight being a 6-0 thrashing of local rivals Bacup in the Combination Cup. Off the field the financial position deteriorated further as gate receipts dropped by £200 over the season averaging just £37, with contributions from the supporters club the only thing keeping the club afloat.

1954-55

With Roland Sharpe appointed director in charge of football matters the club gambled by investing in eleven professionals and also appointed Sam Horrocks as groundsman. New signings included full back Ron Rothwell from Rochdale, winger William Cowsill from Darwen and Burnley juniors Edmund Hartley and Harry Evans.

The season opened with two defeats against the reserve sides of league clubs Oldham and Accrington Stanley. A 3-0 win over Marine got the season up and running and although the club struggled to put a run together the impressive forward line produced enough wins to keep the club in the pack chasing runaway leaders Accrington Stanley reserves. One highlight of this period was the 4 goals scored by local amateur Brian Nuttall in the 5-4 win over Southport reserves whilst on leave from national service all done in white boots, probably one of the first cases of coloured boots in the country. The club further strengthened the side picking up forward Joe Slattery from Morecambe and one of the country's leading amateur golfers Hugh Lewis who was also a talented inside forward.

The club embarked on a run of nine wins in ten games to establish themselves at the head of a group of four teams chasing leader s Accrington. A run of one point from three games after Easter ended any hopes the club had of catching Accrington reserves. However, back to back 9-1 wins over South Liverpool and Netherfield secured runners up spot and ensured the club finished leading scorers with 123 goals with Willie Brown and Eddie Hartley both scoring over 20 goals.

Only the Junior Cup brought any cup success as Chorley and Droylesden were overcome to set up a semi-final at Nelson the club forced a replay, but Rossy lost 2-1 before a gate of £122 to bow out of the competition. The club's gamble did improve gates with an average of £51 a big improvement from the previous season but once again the club were heavily dependent on the Supporters club to keep the club solvent.

1955-56

With the only changes from the squad that finished runners up being the loss of leading scorer Willie Brown who was replaced by Tommy Willighan from Burnley reserves and with Jack Buchanan coming in from Nelson, the club were confident of once again making a challenge for the Championship.

However, with Hugh Lewis not available till October due to his professional golfing commitments in Sweden and several injuries, the club made a slow start to the season. A good run in October and November saw the club rise to seventh in the league. Unfortunately, Steve Molloy broke his leg in the game with Chorley and the selection committees chopping and changing of the team saw results suffer.

A run of five consecutive defeats after Christmas saw the club slide down the table. A vital win over bottom club St Helens stopped the rot but the club lost all three games over Easter to slip back into trouble. Back to back wins over Fleetwood and Morecambe gave the club hope, however defeat at third bottom Bacup saw the clubs swap places. This was one of five defeats that finished the season and saw the club slip into the bottom two on the last day of the season as South Liverpool won to move above them and consign Rossy to second division football for the first time in over 40 years.

The club did enjoy its best FA Cup run for six years beating Droylesden and Chorley to reach the third qualifying round before losing to Ashton Utd, but other cup competitions were disappointing, apart from a 9-2 win over Leyland Motors in the Junior cup first round.

1956-57

In preparation to their first season of second division football since before WWI the club made several changes, former player Ron Rothwell was made trainer and only five professionals were retained, Johnny Clark, Derek Hughes, Jack Buchanan, Tommy Willighan, and Harry Evans. New signings included former Bacup and Stalybridge forward Frank Campbell, and goalkeeper Brian Sutton from Rochdale.

The season opened with an 8-2 win at Earlestown Rossendale second biggest opening day win, however in typical Rossendale style this was followed by a shock 1-0 home defeat by Clitheroe. The club then lost young forward Peter Greenwood who was signed by Bury, the club acted swiftly bringing in experienced forward Geoff Cookson from Fleetwood.

The club then embarked on an eleven match unbeaten run to establish themselves in the promotion places. A club record run of fourteen consecutive league wins between the beginning of December and the end of March saw the club move well clear at the top of the table. A 5-1 win over Burscough reserves on the 19th of April secured the Championship and promotion with four games to play and the club eventually finished eight points clear of closest rivals Crompton Recreation to secure a return to the Lancashire combination top flight.

The cub also enjoyed success in cup competitions after an early exit in the FA Cup, the club defeated Bacup Great Harwood and Nelson to reach the semi-finals of the Combination Cup before losing to Horwich RMI. The club went one better in the Junior Cup beating Padiham, Lytham, South Liverpool and Darwen to set up a final against New Brighton at Ewood Park. The club battled gamely against their higher ranked opponents before losing 1-0 to a Mycock header on the hour. Earlier in the season the club had won the North East Lancashire Charity Cup beating Clitheroe 6-0 in the final at Accrington stanley's Peel Park ground, this was the first time the club had played a competitive game under floodlights.

This marked the clubs most successful season since the 1920's and this success was reflected off the field with league gates averaging £40, the coffers also being boosted by several big gates in the cup competitions.

1957-58

With most of the squad available that won promotion the club added winger Tommy Powdrill from Lytham, plus amateurs keeper Ken Bland and winger Bill O Laughlin from Bury.

The season opened with a creditable draw with Wigan athletic and a five game unbeaten run before a loss to Accrington Stanley Reserves. Three more wins were reeled off to move into the top three. The club then struggled to put a consistent run together the inconsistency highlighted in the festive fixtures that saw the club win 6-3 at Chorley on Christmas day before losing the return game at Dark Lane 6-0 on Boxing Day. The club entered the new year in sixth place but a run of just one win in nine games in the new year ended any championship ambitions. The club finished the season quite strongly to secure a creditable eighth placed finish upon their return to the top flight of the Lancashire Combination.

The club had little cup success falling at the first hurdle in the FA Cup and in the second round of the Combination Cup and Junior Cups, the club did however successfully defend the NE Lancashire charity Cup beating Accrington Stanley reserves 6-1 in the final at Dark Lane. At the end of the season a special committee was set up to undertake ground improvements especially with regard to the drainage of the playing surface.

1958-59

The only addition to the professional ranks was winger Jimmy Birkett from Netherfield, but it was amateur centre forward Derek Hutchinson who caught the eye in an opening day win over Oldham reserves, his early season form was to earn him county trials before injury ended his season, he was later to become chairman of the club in the 1980's.

The club had to wait till the end of September for their next league win and found themselves struggling at the wrong end of the table. The club then went on a run of improved form that saw the club move up to eleventh position as Christmas approached. The highlight of this period was an 11-2 win over Fleetwood that saw young Rossendale amateur Clifford Greaves score 6 goals on his debut. His eleven goals in his first four games earned Greaves trials at Blackpool and Accrington Stanley. The club then endured a miserable festive period losing all four games to slip down the table. Bad weather then saw no games played for four weeks and the rest seemed to do Rossy good as they then embarked on a six match unbeaten run, however this was followed by six straight defeats before four wins from five games secured a sixteenth place finish well clear of relegated Clitheroe and Droylesden.

The FA Cup and Junior Cups brought little success, however the club did enjoy a run in the Combination cup beating Clitheroe, Nelson and New Brighton to set up a semi final meeting with Horwich RMI for the second time in three years and once again the Grundy Hill slope was to prove decisive as the club were well beaten 3-0.

On the financial front there had been a dramatic decline in gate receipts to just £860 for the season and despite the usual sterling contribution from the supporters club a loss of £199 was made on the season. However, Chairman Billy Holden continued to invest in the club as over the close season the cover opposite the grandstand was refurbished, a new turnstile block built and most importantly the much needed work on the playing surface was undertaken.

1959-60

Rossendale were optimistic of improving on the disappointment of previous seasons after adding full back Sam Anderson from Oldham, the vastly experienced Tom Dryburgh from Morecambe who had played over 200 league games with clubs such as Leicester City and Hull and Scottish forward Bob Scott who did not settle with Lancaster after leaving Bacup and returned to the valley with dramatic results.

The club made a steady start to the season and with Scott finding the net at regular intervals the club were firmly established in the leading pack. The club were fifth going into the Christmas period nine points behind runaway leaders Chorley with the mercurial Bob Scott leading the way with 32 goals in the first twenty league games. Unfortunately, the club were conceding nearly as many goals as they scored and former Man City and Bury reserve Kingsley Davies was brought in to replace veteran Derek Hughes. Rossendale also lost exciting winger Bill O Laughlin to Oldham at the end of January. None of this seemed to unsettle Scott who continued to find the net regularly to ensure Rossendale finished the season in fifth place eighteen points behind Champions Chorley. The club scored 116 goals but conceded 95 with Bob Scott contributing 51 of those goals he also scored 21 cup goals to smash the club record for a season of 56 by John Williams during the 1928/29 season.

The FA Cup and Combination cups brought little success but the club did enjoy a good run in the Junior Cup beating beating Northern Nomads, Horwich RMI and Bacup to set up a semi-final at favourites Chorley despite Scott scoring his twelfth goal of the competition Rossy went down 2-1. Despite the goal fest of a season gates dropped once again to an average of just £35 a game and once again it was the efforts of the Supporters club plus the goodwill of Chairman Billy Holden that kept the club going.

1960-61

The club brought in new players Tommy Appleton from Accrington Stanley, Vince Marren from Ashton Utd and Alan Clarke from Colwyn Bay for the new season and the club were also boosted financially when Beverley Beers agreed to sponsor the covered accommodation at the ground.

Once again, the club were indebted to prolific striker Bob Scott who scored three hat tricks in his first five games to keep Rossy in the top half of the table. A run of four wins in November saw the club reach a highpoint of fourth in the table six points behind leaders Nelson, but this run was ended by an 11-2 thrashing at Ashton Utd.

The club were comfortably positioned in eighth going into the new year but despite Scott's goals the club were to manage only two further league victories as they slid down the league to finish sixteenth, the low point of this run was undoubtedly a 10-2 home defeat to struggling Earlstown. The club managed to concede fifty goals in their last ten games to finish with the worst defensive record in the whole league conceding 139 goals in 42 league games.

Once again despite early exits in the FA Cup and this time the Junior Cup the club battled through to a semi-final, this time in the Combination Cup where Bacup, Padiham and South Liverpool were defeated to set up a tie against Netherfield the contest went to three replays before Netherfield finally won through 6-1 at Chorley's Victory Park.

1961-62

After the disappointments of last season, the club acted to correct the problems bringing in Scotsman Charlie Ferguson in as player coach who had league experience with Hamilton Academicals, Accrington Stanley, Rochdale and Oldham, he was to work with a three man selection committee including new board member Bob Davies a Bury Councillor.

Ferguson brought in full back Andy Kirkaldy from Bacup and winger Eric Betts from Earlstown and goalkeeper Alan Guinn from Oldham. The club lost the first three games but a 3-2 win over champions Chorley in front of a £50 gate kick started the season and a nine match unbeaten run saw the club rise up to sixth by the end of November. Although the club did not repeat this consistency a more settled pattern off team selection paid dividends and a run of five wins in April secured a sixth place finish for the club.

Unfortunately, there was no cup success this year as the club failed to win a single cup game.

Back Row (left to right):   S. Molloy, A. Kirkaldy, G. Winn, A. Guinn, D. Ormerod, K. Davies.

Front Row (left to right):   J. Clark, T. Willighan, T. Appleton, C. Ferguson, R. Scott, E. Betts.

1962-63

The only new signing for the start of the season was former Rochdale winger Jimmy Brown from Altrincham. Any hopes of building on last seasons improvements were soon dashed as four of the first five league games were lost including two 8-1 defeats at Netherfield and Horwich.

The club then went on a six match unbeaten run to move away from the bottom of the table. The defensive frailties were all to evident and Charlie Fergusons involvement with the club ended in the new year, but results did not improve. The big freeze meant only one game was played between the 15th December and the 27th February when a rusty Rossendale slumped to an 11-0 defeat at Morecambe.

Once winter relented the games came thick and fast and Rossy like many teams struggled to cope turning out with just ten men at Marine and veteran defender Johnny Clark found himself keeping goal on three occasions. This did provide opportunities for some, like schoolboy Colin Blant whose performances earned him a contract at Burnley FC.

The forward line of Scott, Willighan and Appleton found goals easy to come by against tired defences in the run in and a run of eight wins from the last ten games in just thirty two days saw the club finish a comfortable fourteenth.

The cup games brought little joy with a solitary FA Cup win over Leyland Motors to show for their efforts. During the season striker Bob Scott established the clubs all time goalscoring record passing two hundred goals in just four seasons. The harsh winter and indifferent form meant the season was a disaster financially the club making a loss of £928, despite a donation from the Supporters club of £2301 over the season. In an effort to cut the annual wage bill of £2592 only six semi-professionals would be used next season.

1963-64

The club retained just three professionals from last season in Clark, Kirkaldy and Ormerod and added local lad Graeme Lord who had league experience with Accy Stanley and played last season as an amateur, Roy Barrett from Bacup and Ian McCrae another former Stanley player were also added to the squad.

The season started poorly, and the club had to wait until their tenth game for their first league win and the club was stuck in the bottom three. It was mid November before Rossy recorded another league win and by this time Chairman Billy Holden had begun to loosen the purse strings bringing in the experienced Paddy Sowden as player coach, former favourite winger Eddie Hartley also returned to the club along with another ex Accy player Gordon Stones. However, the results did not make an immediate improvement and Christmas arrived with Rossy having just twelve points from twenty one games and lying in eighteenth position.

The club then received a massive boost with the return to the club of record goalscorer Bob Scott from Nelson and he did not disappoint marking his return with a hat trick in a 3-2 win over former club Nelson helping Rossy complete a Christmas double over their neighbours. With Scott leading the line the club began to climb clear of the relegation zone eventually finishing sixteenth well clear of the bottom two.

This successful end to the season also saw a young David Lloyd make an impact at the club with three goals in his nine appearances before leaving to concentrate on his cricket career. There was no joy in cup competitions as the club fell at the first hurdle in all three competitions. Off the field there was no improvement in the financial position as gates dropped by an average of £7 per game on the previous season.

1964-65

At the club AGM secretary Roland Sharpe announced that the priority for the club was to clear debts and to this end only six semi pros were retained, when Bob Scott was enticed away by Horwich RMI the club brought in former Prescot centre forward Peter Blease.

Once again, the club started the season disastrously with just one point from their first six games. The club then recorded their first win against Droylesden but after ten games the club were third from bottom with just four points. The signings of Brian Nuttall and Ted Duxberry saw some improvement and with Blease finding the net regularly the club moved up one place and a run of four wins leading up to Boxing Day moved the club clear of the bottom three and gave them some breathing space. The club guaranteed safety with a 4-0 win over next to bottom Accrington in April and eventually finished eighteenth, fourteen points clear of relegation.

The season also saw Johnny Clark complete his seven hundred and fiftieth appearance for the club. In the FA Cup Great Harwood were beaten 1-0 before Stalybridge proved too strong winning 3-0 in the second qualifying round, Marine despatched Rossy in the first round of the Junior Cup. The club had more success in the Combination Cup seeing off Nelson and Darwen after replays before losing 4-2 at Chorley.

Off the field the financial position of the club was not helped by a fire in the main stand in November and an appeal was launched to raise money to repair the damage, this eventually raised £363 the old stand was repaired and refurbished but with a reduced capacity of 450.

1965-66

With the financial situation still tight the club made Paddy Sowden player manager and started the season with just six semi-professionals Terry Kenyon joining from Bacup and local goalkeeper Peter Vipham from Chorley were added to retained pros Dennis Ormerod, Gordon Stones, Brian Nuttall and Paddy Sowden. The clubs aim was to concentrate on local amateurs and develop young talent.

The season opened with a 0-0 draw with Skelmersdale the clubs first 0-0 draw at Dark Lane since 26th November 1955. However, after six games the club were rooted to the foot of the table with just three points, things did improve slowly and a four match unbeaten run saw them rise to seventeenth. This was a highpoint in the season as a winless run of eight games saw them slip back into a relegation dogfight with six other teams including local rivals Bacup and Nelson. The club gained a vital league win over Bacup but were still in deep trouble at the beginning of May. Wins over relegation rivals Southport reserves and a 5-0 thrashing of Fleetwood in the penultimate game of the season guaranteed safety. This was just as well as the last game of the season at home to Leyland was abandoned at half time with the club losing 1-0 due to a hail storm, as nothing was at stake the result was allowed to stand.

The clubs FA Cup tie with Darwen was delayed and eventually played with no away support as the town was quarantined after a polio outbreak. Rossy forced a replay in the next round at Chorley but lost the replay 3-0, they were boosted by a gate of £65 the clubs highest for five years. In other cup competitions the club exited in the first round.

1966-67

The club lengthened the pitch by 3 yards prior to the season and manager Paddy Sowden's main signings were the experienced Stan Howard from Chorley, Forward Mick Muldoon from Padiham and full back Billy McGinn from Oldham, whilst Brian Nuttall and Ted Duxberry left the club for Bacup.

The season opened with a 4-2 defeat at Guinness Exports a game that saw Barry Harrison become Rossendale first ever substitute. Four more defeats followed and this saw Rossy firmly rooted to the foot of the table with Great Harwood and Darwen. The club finally recorded their first league win against Leyland on the 13th September. Vital wins over relegation rivals Darwen, Great Harwood and Guiness Exports saw Rossy finish the year in nineteenth position. A winless run of nine games saw Rossy slip back into the bottom two before a Chris Chesworth penalty earned Rossy a crucial 1-0 win over Darwen. As the season entered its final stretch the club were still in deep trouble but boosted by an influx of Leeds University students friends of player David Klemm, Rossy finished the season with a seven match unbeaten run to finish safely in eighteenth position.

In the FA Cup Rossy overcame Burscough before losing to Lancaster City after a replay, Burscough gained their revenge knocking Rossy out of the Junior Cup at the first hurdle. Rossendale did enjoy success in the Combination Cup defeating Droylesden and Bacup before pulling off a highly creditable 2-0 win at Marine in the Quarter finals with a very young makeshift team due to most of the current squad being cup tied. Unfortunately, Fleetwood proved too strong for Rossy winning the semi-final 2-1.

At the end of the season manager Sowden announced his resignation to take up a scouting role with Blackpool as the club once again faced financial difficulties with gates dropping alarmingly to as low as £12 for the visit of Clitheroe and only four semi-professionals were retained.

Back row: K Battersby, G Stones, C Chesworth, S Howard, B Harrison, P Vipham.

Front row: G Greenwood, M Muldoon, D Ormrod(capt), L Dagger, D Klemm.

1967–68

Gordon Stones was appointed player manager to replace Paddy Sowden and new signings included keith Tomlinson from Nelson and Richard Stewart from Rochdale, whilst Brian Nuttall and Peter Blease both returned to Dark Lane. The club had new floodlight bulbs installed and entered the Lancashire Floodlight cup, hoping the increased midweek games would improve gates.

The season opened with a 3-0 defeat at fancied Skelmersdale, a win over Droylesden followed but two heavy defeats including a record breaking 14-0 drubbing at Morecambe set alarm bells ringing. The team however bounced back well with just one defeat in the next five to move the club up to twelfth. A run of seven consecutive defeats then saw the club slide down the table into the relegation places. A vital 4-0 win over bottom club Prescot at the beginning of December lifted the gloom. This was followed by four more defeats including a Christmas double against struggling Wigan Rovers. Bad weather meant the club played no league games in January but when the weather relented a 4-2 defeat at home to Southport reserves saw the club slip to the bottom of the league. A 3-1 win over local rivals Clitheroe failed to improve the position and manager Stones tendered his resignation, the club acted swiftly bringing in Les Rigby initially as player coach before appointing him manager towards the end of the season.

There was no improvement in results as only two more games were won before the end of the season as the club remained rooted to the foot of the table. Events off the field meant the club knew they were safe from relegation well before the end of the season due to the formation of the Northern Premier League and the subsequent loss of clubs making the Lancashire Combination operate just one division for the following season.

Cup competitions brought little joy with heavy defeats bringing first round exits in the FA cup and Junior cup, the club did defeat Droylesden in the Combination cup before bowing out in the next round. The much heralded Floodlight cup proved a damp squib as Ashton Utd were overcome in the first round but this was followed by a 9-2 aggregate defeat against Chorley and the money the new competition generated failed to pay the cost of the new floodlight bulbs.

The financial situation showed no sign of improvement despite the cost cutting measures with gates down to an average of just £11. The club were honoured however when long serving secretary and vice chairman Roland Sharpe was appointed President of the Lancashire Combination.

1968-69

Les Rigby strengthened his squad during the summer bringing in experienced goalkeeper Neil Kirby from Worcester City, young midfielder Terry Lane from Bacup, Alan Holden from Runcorn and young winger David Crompton who had been playing as an amateur at Rochdale.

The club made their best start to a season for over ten years with three wins and a draw from the first four games to challenge at the top of the table. Three defeats followed and by the end of September the club had slipped to fourteenth, results did improve but consistency remained elusive. Several signings were made to improve the side most importantly Peter Bourne the former Colne Dynamo on his release from Burnley and Johnny Pearson from Wigan Rovers. The club had to be content with a thirteenth place finish but the team were starting to play some attractive football and in Pearson, Bourne and Crompton had the basis of a forward line that augured well for the future.

The cup competitions again offered little, Bacup were overcome in the FA cup before Witton Albion once again ended our interest, Wigan Rovers were defeated in the first round of the Combination cup before a defeat at Great Harwood put us out, whilst the Junior cup and Floodlight cup saw first round exits.

Off the field the cost cutting measures were starting to take effect as the deficit was cut to £634 and gate receipts were up £71 to £591 for the season. Concerns were expressed though at the weakness of the combination due to the exodus of teams to the NPL and Cheshire leagues.

1969-70

Manager Les Rigby continued to ring the changes prior to the season in order to strengthen the team. In came centre half Bob Woods from Chorley, forward John Bond from Morecambe, keeper Tony Unsworth from Burscough and Jimmy Howard from Bacup. Also, Tommy Nuttall returned to the club from Bacup as trainer.

The season opened with a 2-0 win over Darwen the clubs first opening day win for over ten years. Five wins out of the first six games saw Rossy handily placed in the top three. The good form continued and a run of five wins to the end of October saw the club mounting a serious challenge for the title for the first time in years. However, a Combination cup defeat to local rivals Bacup who were also enjoying their best season for some years brought a temporary slump in form and the club fell behind the leading pack. Ironically, a Boxing Day win over Bacup sparked an unbeaten run of nine league games that brought the club back into contention, this was built on a fine run of form by striker Johnny Pearson who scored a total of twenty goals in a club record nineconsecutive league and cup games. A shock defeat at Wigan athletic reserves followed by a controversial 1-0 reverse at title rivals Chorley effectively ended the clubs title challenge and the season petered out with three defeats to finish a disappointing seventh well behind Champions Burscough.

Over the course of the season manager Rigby continued to strengthen the team bringing experienced defender Roy Wilkinson from Netherfield and winger Jimmy Hammill from Chorley. The club also enjoyed more success in cup competitions getting beyond the first hurdle in all the cups, but it was the Junior cup that the club excelled in, defeating Lytham and Burscough in the first two rounds to set up a quarter final tie at Morecambe, the team earned a replay with a hard fought 1-1 draw before thrashing their Northern Premier League rivals 5-2 in the replay thanks to four goals from Pearson. This set up a semi-final with Wigan at Springfield Park and the club were unlucky to lose a tight game 2-1.

Off the field the club were rocked by the death of long serving Vice Chairman and former secretary Rowland Sharpe in October, this was followed in March by the shock announcement that the club was resigning from the Lancashire Combination to apply for membership of the Cheshire league. This did not meet with the approval of a large section of supporters and manager Les Rigby had to take part in a series of meetings and press articles to convince fans that the change was necessary to ensure better quality football and the continued development of the football club.

1970-71

With the step up in the standard expected with the move to the Cheshire League Les Rigby made several signings, bringing in the vastly experienced Alan Kirkman as player assistant manager, full back David Wild from Radcliffe, former Wigan and Altrincham centre back Dennis Crompton, Scots midfielder

Billy Greenan from Bacup, centre forward Glyn Barker from Great Harwood and utility player Kenny Fletcher from Droylesden.

The season opened with a hard fought draw at Nantwich then the club went on a run of eight consecutive wins to top the league and have the crowds flocking back to Dark Lane as several four figure gates were recorded. The unbeaten start to the season was extended to nineteen games before a surprise 4-0 defeat at Horwich on the 19th December ended the clubs record breaking start to a season. A couple of draws saw the club slip to second behind defending champions Skelmersdale, but a 1-0 win at Marine at the beginning of January saw the club return to the top and despite a 3-0 reverse to Burscough which established them as Rossy's main rivals for the title the club never relinquished top spot again.

A competitive Easter period that brought four points from a possible six to virtually ensure the Championship, which was confirmed with a 2-2 draw against Port Vale reserves on the 17th April. The club added the Cheshire League challenge Shield with a 3-0 win over Burscough a week later.

The club entered a record six cup competitions playing a mammoth twenty four cup ties over the season, they enjoyed some success in the FA cup beating St Helens and Horwich to reach the third qualifying round for the first time since 1955 before losing to South Liverpool. They exited the FA trophy at the first hurdle losing to Horden CW, their first ever meeting with a Northern league team. They also bowed out early in the Cheshire League Cup and Lancashire Floodlight Cup. Once again the Junior Cup saw the club enjoy a good run defeating Nelson and Bacup before beating NPL Fleetwood in the quarter final after two replays to set up another semi-final against Wigan Athletic who again won narrowly 1-0 at Springfield Park.

The club had also entered the Lancs FA floodlight League cup and won their group which contained Bacup, Milnethorpe Corinthians and Great Harwood to set up a two legged semi-final against Fleetwood which Rossy won comfortably 5-2 on aggregate. The Final was played over two legs against Kirkby Town and Rossy assured themselves of silver ware winning the first leg at Kirkby 7-1, although the seventh goal was highly dubious a disgruntled Kirkby fan diverting the ball into the Kirkby goal just before the final whistle. The second leg was an anti-climax which Kirkby won 2-1. The 8-3 aggregate win saw the first piece of cup silver ware enter the Dark Lane boardroom since the NE Lancashire cup was won in 1958. The marathon season ended on a high note with 3 pieces of silver ware in the trophy cabinet to end the clubs best ever season.

The club had played a total of sixty seven competitive games with skipper Bob Woods playing in all but two of them whilst the front three of John Pearson, Glyn Barker and Peter Bourne had scored a 102 goals between them. The only cloud on the horizon was a disappointing drop in gates from the start of the season which had seen several £150 plus gates, to gates averaging just half that amount on the run in to the title, raising the question not for the first or last time, did the valley really want to support a top class football team.

The successful 1970–71 squad.

Back row :   Tommy Nuttall (trainer), Tony Unsworth, Glyn Barker, Eddie Birchall, Dennis Crompton, John Wood, David Wild, Roy Wilkinson, Charlie Wroth, Wally Roberts, Les Rigby(managr).

Front row: Kenny Fletcher, Peter Bourne, John Pearson, Bob Woods, Billy Greenan, David Crompton, Jimmy Hammill.

1971-72

With Roy Wilkinson retiring and Peter Bourne's departure to Australia imminent Les Rigby brought in left back Dave Hoolickin from Ashton Utd, forward John Clay from Macclesfield and defender Fred Eyre from Fleetwood.

Rossendale's defence of the Cheshire League Championship began badly with three defeats in the first four games, before five wins from the next six games saw the club challenging at the top end of the table. The club then struggled for consistency as they became distracted by their success in the FA Cup and the club entered the Christmas period well off the pace, but with several games in hand.

Form improved in the new year and after a shock 7-3 defeat at Witton in January the club boosted by new signings Jimmy Lynn from Netherfield and Tommy Ross from Sligo Rovers in Ireland, put together a run of ten consecutive victories to emerge as leaders Rhyl's closest challengers. As the hectic fixture list, eighteen games in seven weeks began to take its toll defeats against Orsmkirk and Mossley meant the club went to Rhyl knowing only a big win would suffice. However, a jaded team fell to a 4-0 defeat to hand the title to their opponents, eventually finishing runners up sixpoints behind Rhyl.

Once again, the club enjoyed great success in cup competitions, after an early exit in the Cheshire league cup, the club embarked on an historic FA cup adventure defeating NPL opponents Netherfield, Morecambe and Lancaster to set up 4th qualifying round tie against Stafford Rangers the top non-league side in the country. In possibly the greatest game ever played at Dark Lane Rossy allowed a 3-1lead to slip away in the closing stages only to hammer home 3 goals in the last five minutes to win 6-3 in front of a record gate of £330. This win saw the club reach the FA cup proper for the first time in its history. Rossy were drawn at home to fellow non leaguers Altrincham, heavy snow meant the original tie was postponed and Altrincham refused to play under Rossendale's floodlights so the tie was played on a Monday afternoon in front of BBC news cameras. A crowd of 1769 saw Rossy win a tight encounter 1-0 thanks to a David wild penalty in the 11th minute. Rossendale's reward was another home game against Bolton Wanderers. The massive interest in the game meant the tie had to be switched to Bury's Gigg Lane ground. A crowd of over 12,000 saw Rossy dominate the early stages and take a 16th minute lead through John Clay. Rossy held their lead until the 43rd minute when Roy Greaves equalised, and within a minute Greaves headed Bolton into a half time lead. When John Byrom made it 3-1 on 50minutes the tie was effectively over Greaves completed his hat trick as Bolton won 4-1 but Rossy gained many plaudits for their plucky display and the club were delighted with their £1445 share of the record £3965 gate receipts. The club also enjoyed a record run in the FA Trophy defeating HorwichRMI, Netherfield and Winsford to set up an away trip to Southern League Burton Albion who proved too strong beating an injury hit Rossy 2-0. The club bowed out of the Junior cup at the quarter final stage losing at home to Netherfield. However, the Floodlight KO cup brought more success to the club as NPL Fleetwood, Great Harwood and Chorley were defeated to set up a two legged final against bogey team Wigan Athletic, a late Billy Greenan goal earned a 2-1 win at Dark Lane and a superb defensive display and a well taken goal by Glyn Barker gave Rossy a well earned 1-0 win at Springfield Park to bring the silver ware back to Dark lane with a 3-1 aggregate win.

Another historically successful season ended with nine teams from the NPL defeated in cup games, but Rossendale's ambitions of playing at a higher level were frustrated by gates flatlining for the bread and butter league games and the financial restraints this imposed. It was a shock the clubs most successful manager in its history chose to accept the Radcliffe job although he moved on to the Wigan Athletic job within weeks.

The Rossendale squad pictured before the historic FA cup tie with Bolton.

Back row: from left Tommy Nuttall(trainer), Kenny Fletcher, Wally Roberts, Dennis Crompton, Dave Hoolickin.

Middle row: John Young, John Clay, John Wood, David Wild, David Crompton.

Front row: Glyn Barker, Fred Eyre, Les Rigby(manager), Bob Woods, Billy Greenan. Ball boys Howard Parker and Brent Peters.

David Wild slots home the penalty that defeats Altrincham and puts Rossy into the FA Cup second round. One of a record breaking 17 he was to convert during the season.

Billy Greenan challenges Bolton keeper Charlie Wright during the FA cup 2nd round tie at Gigg Lane.

1972-73

Rossy promoted Les Rigby's assistant Alan Kirkman to the manager role and the pre-season Ashworth Cup between the winners of the Lancashire FA's Junior and Floodlight Cups saw Rossy renew acquaintances with their former manager, Rossy won both legs to win 4-1 on aggregate and bring yet more silverware to Dark Lane.

Rossy started the season disastrously, failing to score in six of the first seven league games and gaining just one win, as the club languished in nineteenth place. Les Rigby returned to his old club to tempt John

Pearson to Wigan for a fee of £500 and manager Kirkman rang the changes as Eyre, Clay and Roberts were all released and Winger Dave Crompton was forced to retire after failing to fully recover from his broken leg. Into the side came midfielders Bernie Baldwin from Bacup and Bobby Grimshaw from Netherfield and winger Dave O Neill from Blackburn, youngsters Derek Sadler and John Cooke were also given opportunities. There was no immediate improvement in results and Christmas arrived with Rossy still stuck at the wrong end of the table. An eight match unbeaten run into the New Year improved Rossendale league position and a run of nine consecutive wins saw the team charge up the table and the strong finish to the season saw the club eventually finish fifth thirteen points behind Champions Buxton.

Rossy's early season problems saw the club exit the FA cup at the first attempt losing 2-1 to Bangor City, although this was in the fourth qualifying round after the previous season exploits. Little progress was made in the other cup competitions apart from the Lancashire Junior Cup where Radcliffe, Darwen and Northern Nomads were overcome to set up a semi-final at Skelmersdale, where a rare Bernie Baldwin goal saw Rossy through to the final.

The final at Ewood Park watched by around 1500 people saw Rossendale meet local rivals Great Harwood and in a tight first half a Kershaw goal gave favourites Harwood a first half lead. Rossendale hit back and dominated the second half equalising through Dave O Neill before Glyn Barker fired home to give Rossy a deserved win and bring the Junior Cup back to Dark Lane for the first time since 1912.

One black mark against the club was on the disciplinary front after keeper John Wood refused to leave the field after being sent off at Witton, forcing the abandonment of the match, bringing himself and the club hefty fines and Wood a three week suspension at the start of the next season.

During the season the new floodlights were opened with a friendly against a strong Burnley team who won 1-0 thanks a Ray Hankin goal.

The Rossendale team pictured before the FA Cup tie with Bangor City.

Back Row: David Wild, Dennis Crompton, Bob Woods, John Wood, Derek Sadler, Tommy Ross and David Crompton.

Front Row: Glyn Barker, Billy Greenan, Jimmy Lynn, Kenny Fletcher and Bernie Baldwin. Ball Boys Howard Parker and Brent Peters.

1973-74

The main signing prior to the new season was the return of star striker John Pearson after his move to Wigan failed to work out for him. Rossy lost the first game of the season at home to Hyde, but Pearson was soon amongst the goals again as Rossy reeled off eight straight wins to top the table. A mini slump in October saw Rossy pick up just one point from five games and lose the lead to Marine. Injuries were having a big impact on the team although they did give manager Kirkman the opportunity to introduce promising young winger Steve Connaghan to the team

The club returned to winning ways in December but were rocked when Pearson was ruled out for the season after a bad knee injury against New Brighton on Boxing Day. This did not stop the club embarking on a twenty two match unbeaten run including twelve consecutive wins to establish Rossy as clear favourites for the title with only Marine in pursuit. A controversial 1-0 defeat at home to Sandbach, the winner coming from a freekick awarded when Rossy keeper was adjudged to have handled the ball outside the area meant the penultimate game of the season at Marine would be a Championship decider with Rossy 2 points clear of Marine, who had a superior goal average. Rossy appeared to have done enough to have earned the all-important point until Marine were awarded a disputed corner in the 87th minute and Edwards forced the ball home during a goal mouth scramble. Both teams won their last games so Rossy had to be content with runners up spot on goal average.

Rossy made early exits in both FA competitions and the Junior Cup but would pick up silver ware in the Cheshire League Cup, where Droylesden, Stalybridge Oldham Reserves and Formby were overcome to set up a two legged final against Burscough. Rossy lost the first leg 3-0 and were given little chance in the return leg, they pulled one goal back before half time and turned in a superb second half performance to score four more goals and win the tie 5-3 on aggregate. Rossendale also added the Lancs FA floodlight Cup to the trophy cabinet beating Chorley and Great Harwood to set up a two legged final against Skelmersdale. Rossy won the first leg after turning in another high octane second half performance scoring four goals in the last twenty two minutes to virtually seal the trophy. The club ensured a 4-0 aggregate victory with an efficient 0-0 draw at Skelmersdale two days later.

This was Rossendale seventh trophy in the four seasons since joining the Cheshire League and Manager Alan Kirkman picked up the manager of the year award for his efforts. Behind the scenes all was not well the Floodlight cup final had brought in gate receipts of just over £80 and long serving Chairman Billy Holden resigned sighting lack of support from the valley as the main reason. He would stay on as club president and major shareholder but wanted new blood on the board of directors.

1974-75

The season opened with yet more silverware as Rossy defeated WiganAthletic 3-1 over two legs to pick up the Ashworth Cup once again. The league season opened with a 3-1 win at Formby but the financial constraints meant Kirkman had been unable to strengthen the squad in the close season and injuries to John Wood, Glyn Barker and Dave Hoolickin meant the club had a difficult start to the season.

The sale of winger Dave O Neill to Huddersfield for £1500 in September eased some of the financial pressure, but only three more league wins saw November arrive with Rossy stuck in the bottom half of the table and out three cup competitions. The board reacted by sacking Alan Kirkman on the 19th November and releasing Dennis Crompton, Bernie Baldwin and Fred Herring to cut the wage bill, Hoolickin and Fitzsimmons were also placed on the transfer list.

Long serving trainer Tommy Nuttall handed in his resignation and Club Captain Bob Woods was made caretaker manager. Not surprisingly the team continued to struggle and Christmas arrived with the club struggling at the wrong end of the table. The Board appointed Don Wilson as the new manager and the former Mossley boss returned to his old club bringing in Kevin Burke as his coach and signing Bruce Birtwistle to help Glyn Barker up front. The club went through February undefeated extending their unbeaten run to eight games to move up the table. Form continued to improve and the manager added John Ryder, Billy Kay and Fred Meadowcroft to his squad as the team eventually in finished in eighth place.

Cup competitions offered little respite as the club suffered early exits in all but the Junior Cup, where the club battled through to the Quarter Finals before losing narrowly to Lancaster.

1975-76

Manager Don Wilson brought in several new signings and appointed Don Partridge as his assistant manager, the main signings were Alan Roberts from Mossley, Local centre forward Ian Warburton after his release by Southport and centre back Steve Waywell from Darwen. One player the manager had not managed to adequately replace was goalkeeper John Wood who joined winger Steve Connaghan at Altrincham now managed by Les Rigby and this proved decisive as Rossy lost three of the first four games conceding eleven goals. Wilson acted swiftly to rectify this problem bringing in former Mossley keeper Geoff Foster and results improved immediately. A six match unbeaten run up to Christmas saw the club reach tenth place eleven points behind leaders Winsford but with three games in hand due to the clubs FA Cup exploits.

After a Boxing Day defeat at Radcliffe the club embarked on a thirteen match unbeaten run that lifted the club into contention at the top end of the table. However, the off field problems were starting to take effect, star striker Glyn Barker had been sold to Horwich, Billy Greenan had left to join Ashton Utd and the experienced Tommy Ross had been released to cut the wage bill. The club won only one of their last fifteen games scoring just three goals in the process as they slid down the table to eventually finish eleventh. The clubs off field problems prompted manager Don Wilson to resign at the end of March and once again Bob Woods stepped into the breach as manager till the end of the season.

The FA cup offered the club a shot of redemption from their financial woes after first round exits in the FA Trophy and Junior Cup. Leyland Motors were thrashed 8-1 in the first qualifying round setting up a derby with Radcliffe Borough, Rossy were held to a 2-2 draw but won the replay 4-1. This set up a third qualifying tie at home to NPL Lancaster City a vital tie for the club given the dire financial situation that had just come to light. The team battled out a 2-1 win thanks to Bobby Grimshaw's 88th minute penalty. The fourth qualifying round draw saw Rossy given a tough tie against Northern league leaders Blyth Spartans and Rossy gained a hard fought 0-0 draw. The prize for winners of the replay was a home tie against Third division Shrewsbury. The replay was watched by over 1200 bringing in much needed gate receipts of £425, Rossy made a dream start Barker turning in Birtwistle's low cross after 10 minutes but the slick passing of their opponents prompted by the skilfull Alder saw Blyth dominate the rest of the half. The second half was a scrappy affair with the Rossy defence superbly marshalled by Woods keeping their opponents at bay to put Rossy into the FA Cup proper for the second time in four years. A crowd of over 3000 saw a hard fought encounter with their league opponents in a tight contest, Shrewsbury scored the decisive goal in the 83rd minute through a powerful header by Bates. Rossy threw everything at their opponents in the closing stages forcing Mulhearn into several saves, controversially Rossy did find the net during a goalmouth scramble only to find the referee had blown the final whistle seconds beforehand.

Rossy's cup interest was then focused on the Cheshire League cup as the club beat Radcliffe and Chorley to set up a quarter final tie at home to Leek Town unfortunately when the tie was played at the end of March and a much changed Rossy side were no match for their opponents and went down 3-1.

The Rossendale team pictured in November 1975:

Back row: Alan Roberts, Kenny Fletcher, Jack Hitchen, Mick Mills, Bob Woods, Billy Kay, Ian Warburton Derek Partridge(trainer).

Front row: John Ryder, Bruce Birtwistle, Billy Greenan, Tommy Ross and Bobby Grimshaw Inset Geoff Forster and Glyn Barker.

Off the field the season saw the clubs dire financial position become public knowledge in October, when club president Billy Holden severed all ties with the club after a stroke probably brought on by the investigation into his business dealings by the tax man. The club was £6000 in debt, £1200 due to the tax man and losing £65 a week with a wage bill of £135. The clubs accountant recommended voluntary liquidation and the local council in an effort to help secure the clubs future entered into unsuccessful negotiations with the holding company, who were owed £600 in rent arrears, to buy the ground. The FA cup run kept the wolf from the door and cost cutting and fund raising activities stabilised the day to day running of the club. Towards the end of the season Billy Holden was taken to court for failure to produce accounts for the period from 1969–1972 and it became clear how much of his own money had supported the clubs success of the previous six seasons. The 1975–76 season was definitely the end of an era and more trials and tribulations would lie ahead.

1976-77

With costs dramatically cut Bobby Grimshaw, Steve Waywell, Alan Roberts and Bruce Birtwistle all left the club in the summer. Manager Bob Woods brought in John Pemberton from Prestwich, Tommy Holt from Bacup, Colin Smith from Darwen and local lad John Pearson from Haslingden.

The season opened with some silverware as Bacup were beaten over two legs in a reformed Roscoe Cup. The league season opened with a hard fought 0-0 Draw with Marine and four wins from the next five games saw the club handily placed in the top four. A run of four league defeats and an early exit from the FA cup saw the board sack Woods bringing former Halifax scout Eric Roberts in mid-October. The new manager introduced several former pros such as Clive McFadzean from Bradford City and most importantly Tommy Veitch after his release by Hartlepool. A run of six games without defeat into December saw the club move up the table, but once Veitch moved to Scotland to join Morton Rossy picked up just two points from the next thirteen games and Roberts was dismissed.

Former Nelson boss John Tomlinson became Rossy's new manager and he brought some stability to team selection and performances improved with several draws, although the winless run was extended to twenty four games before Rhyl were beaten in the last game of the season. This disastrous run had seen the club slip to 20th the worst finish for nine seasons. The club had a poor season in cup competitions make first round exits in all competitions although their exit in the league cup came after the club were expelled for playing an ineligible player Tommy Veitch in a second replay with Darwen.

1977-78

Manager John Tomlinson brought in a host of new signings, several with football league experience such as Tommy Walker ex Stoke, Don Tobin ex Rochdale and local lad Mick Higgins who had been at Workington during their last season in the football league, added to these were full back Don Rankin who had returned north from Dorchester, young centre half Ian Whitelegg who had been released by Crewe and winger Martin Farnworth from Darwen.

The season started with two defeats but four wins from the next five games saw the club climb the table and a 4-0 win over Droylesden at the end of September saw the club reach a high of fifth. A run of eight games without a win saw the club slide into mid table and gates decline, with the supporters club closed finances became difficult and the players agreed to forego their wages for several weeks. A run of three wins in December and January saw the club move up the table but poor weather and postponements saw the financial position worsen and manager Tomlinson had enough resigning towards the end of February, followed by all the players apart from the ever loyal Bob Woods.

Woods was made manager and given less than a week to raise a team to face league leaders Marine. His first team included a Hockey player and a Rugby player and were hammered 14-2. With no money he blooded several local youngsters such as Wes Dean and Glen Clawson and even got old pal Man City legend Francis Lee to come out of retirement for one game. Woods gradually strengthened the team bringing experienced full back Jack Hitchen back to the club and bringing in a young Mick Gardiner after his release by Preston. After ten defeats New Brighton were beaten 2-0, a run of five defeats followed but the season finished on a high note with two wins and a draw all against top five placed sides to finish 20th.

There was a little cup joy as Lytham were beaten in the FA cup before highly rated Runcorn narrowly won at Dark Lane in the next round. There was first round exits in the FA Trophy and League cup, whilst Nelson were beaten in the first round of the Junior Cup to set up a home tie with a football league bound Wigan Athletic at a snowy Dark Lane Rossy worked hard for creditable 1-1 draw, Wigan scored three goals in the first five minutes in the replay and eventually won 7-0. There was some silverware as Bacup were beaten 5-0 in the Roscoe Cup, all these cup games being played before the exodus of players in February.

The one up side of the highly publicised problems, was a reformed boards attempt to bring expenditure into line with income which should be made easier after the re-opening of the social club and the loyal band of supporters rallied around with several fund raising schemes to give some hope for the future.

The Rossendale squad pictured before the start of the ill fated 1977–78 season.

1978-79

With very little money available to strengthen the squad manager Bob Woods brought in young goalkeeper John Pengelly and defender Chris McKay from Prestwich and forward Gary Schofield from Stockport.

The season opened with three heavy defeats before Radcliffe were beaten 1-0 at Stainton Park. A run of four games undefeated at the end of September lifted the club away from the bottom of the table. This showed the club could compete with the teams around them in the bottom half of the table, but they were often out classed by the top sides, a situation that was quite common in the days before the non-league pyramid. This resulted in some severe thrashings. A run of five defeats at the end of the year that saw just three goals scored and twenty eight conceded proved too much for manager Woods and he tendered his resignation.

A mini ice age then set in that saw no league games played for seven weeks and the Junior cup tie at Blackpool Mechanics postponed five times. This gave the board some breathing space as they deliberated over who to appoint as manager and they eventually appointed Tony Webber as player manager at the end of February. Webber a very experienced forward who had been an FA Trophy winner with Morecambe brought in Tom Ferber as his assistant and they had an instant impact as Ashton Utd and Radcliffe were both defeated to maintain a cushion between Rossy and the bottom three. Webber brought in Martin Scholes from Penrith and Fred Wilkinson from Netherfield to strengthen the squad and performances improved steadily as the club became more competitive and enough points were taken from the sides around them to ensure the team finished 19th well clear of the bottom three.

After the events of the previous season the club were excluded from the senior FA competitions and so they only had the League cup and Junior Cups to compete in. They suffered a first round defeat in the league cup at Accrington Stanley, but made progress in the Junior Cup thrashing Atherton Collieries 8-1 in the first round before beating Blackpool Mechanics 2-1. This set up a quarter final tie at NPL Netherfield and a hard fought 0-0 draw set up a replay at Dark Lane. This proved to be a remarkable game as Netherfield forced the game into extra time with a last minute equaliser and led 4-2 going into injury time at the end of extra time before Micky Gardiner with a 25 yard pile driver and then Lawrie McMahon with a scrambled goal with the last kick of the game forced another replay. Rossy won the toss for venue and eventually won the tie 2-1 again after extra time thanks to a brace form Graham Walton. This set up a semi-final with Chorley who proved too strong for Rossy and won comfortably in the end by 3-0.

Off the field there was some good news with the reopened supporters club proving a success and bringing the promise of a reliable income stream for the future.

1979-80

The season opened in a spirit of optimism for the first time in several years and with manager Webber strengthening the squad, bringing in goalkeeper Phil Critchley from Wigan, defenders Andy Williams and Chris Taylor from the Manchester league and striker Gary Haworth from Prestwich.

The season opened with the team playing an exciting brand of attacking football, but defensive frailties meant the first four league games were all drawn, the club then lost 4-3 at home to Radcliffe, before bouncing back with an unbeaten run of six games that saw the club climb up the table. The year ended with the just two league defeats and the club handily placed behind the leading pack in seventh place with plenty of games in hand due to a good FA cup run.

Things began to go badly wrong in the New Year with three defeats before a couple of draws appeared to steady the ship then a horrendous 8-0 thrashing at Hyde where the defence disintegrated alarmingly set the tone. March ended with a disastrous run of four heavy defeats including 5-0 and 7-0 hammerings at Dark Lane by Burscough and St Helens and manager Webber's position became untenable and he resigned.

The club acted promptly bringing in former Darwen manager Glyn Watson as the new boss and he immediately moved to strengthen the defence by bringing back Gerry Luchka and signing giant centre half Dave Oldfield. This had an instant impact as seven clean sheets were kept in the last twelve games as the club finished the season strongly in 11th place their best finish for several years.

The club exited the League and Junior cups at the first attempt but enjoyed more success in the FA Cup where Lytham were overcome after a replay and Penrith and Curzon Ashton were both despatched to set up a third qualifying round tie with Burscough who proved too good on the day winning 4-0 to send a large crowd of 331 home disappointed.

Off the field the club suffered a blow in August when they were fined £125 by the FA over irregularities over the signing of manager Tony Webber as a player the previous season. However due to a good FA cup run and improved performances there had been a small increase in attendances and with the reopened social club providing regular income the financial position of the club appeared to have stabilised.

The Rossendale team at the start of the 1979–80 season:

Back row: Taylor, Williams, Burland, Scholes, Critchley, Walton, Webber (player manager), Ferber(coach).

Front row: Wilkinson, Haworth, Gardiner, O Kane, Baines.

1980-81

With the financial position continuing to improve, under the leadership of one of football's first Chairwomen Dorothy Heyworth, the re-established social club had enabled the board to turn a deficit of £14000 into a small surplus.

Manager Glyn Watson continued to strengthen the team, bringing back the experienced defender Dave Brookes and young prospect Chris Lilley from the Manchester league along with forwards Bob Taylor from the Bolton Combination and namesake John Taylor from Darwen.

The season opened with a hard earned point at Kirkby Town, but injuries and suspensions meant Watson struggled to put out a regular line up and performances suffered and a run of five defeats in November saw the club slip to 15th. The signing of former Darwen keeper Fred Roberts and centre back Dave Hodgson brought some stability and result improved. Consistency however remained elusive and the club remained rooted in lower mid table but well clear of relegation trouble.

However, the end of the season was overshadowed by the threat of eviction from Dark Lane by the Holding company set up to protect the ground for the club. Prompted by Director Norman Slater the Holding Company gained a court order to remove Rossendale United from the ground and replace them with Rossendale Amateurs. The club vowed to fight on and after frantic negotiations after a ground share at Bacup fell through negotiated a ground share at Droylesden. After public support for a ground fund the club decided to appeal so they could at least start next season at Dark Lane.

There was little cup success as the club missed out in both FA competitions after throwing away leads in the home ties before losing the replays at Worksop and Accrington Stanley. Whilst lowly Prestwich pulled off a shock first[t] round win in the Junior Cup. Droylesden were overcome in the League cup before a defeat by Nantwich ended interest in the competition.

1981-82

The preseason was overshadowed by the impending court case and the club was given notice to quit Dark Lane by the 7th August, however the club won a stay of execution of two weeks at the High Court in London so they could start the season at Dark Lane. Negotiations enabled the club to stay at Dark Lane until the end of September when a judge ruled they had to quit the ground and handover to Rossendale Amateurs. With a hearing set for December the club then had to play home games at Droylesden.

On the pitch the club had added some experience to the team with the signing of centre half Dave Swarbrick from Burscough and Les Brown from Chorley. The season opened with the customary draw and a large crowd witnessed another draw against champions Nantwich at Dark Lane the following Tuesday.

Manager Glyn Watson had the team playing attractive attacking football and with the pacy young forward Mark Capstick in the goals the club were handily positioned in 6th place at the end of September when they left Dark Lane. Watson continued to strengthen the squad bringing in experienced centre half

Steve Murfin and pacey winger Derek Farnsworth both from St Helens. The club reeled off seven consecutive wins between mid-October and January to move up to third behind leaders Chorley, before a run of three points from seven games ended any Championship ambitions. The club boosted by the news they had finally settled the dispute with the holding company moved back to Dark Lane for Easter and finished the season strongly with just one defeat in their last eight games to end the season in a highly creditable fifth place.

The club bowed out at the first hurdle in the FA Cup, League Cup and Lancashire Junior Cup, but enjoyed a record equalling run in the FA Trophy in very trying circumstances. Northern League West Auckland Town and Ferryhill were overcome before the third qualifying tie with Penrith coincided with the worst of the winter weather and was postponed nine times. The game was switched to Mossley's ground to beat the weather, the move paid off as Rossy won 3-1 to set up a first round tie at Buxton, where a last minute winner from Wilson set up a trip to Isthmian league champions Slough. Rossy performed very well at their more illustrious opponents and were desperately unlucky to lose to a hotly disputed penalty.

The season had finished on a high note on the pitch but off it the club had to pick up the pieces of their battle to win back Dark Lane. As part of the agreement that had seen the club get a 999 year lease and take control of the board of the Holding company through appointment of Clifford Barcroft club president and Peter Horton club auditor to the board. The club had to pick up all the legal costs of over £15000.

With the club failing to get a good enough ground grading for the newly formed North West Counties League top division, the club had also lost another floodlight pylon to high winds whilst they had been off the ground meaning the lights were no longer fit for matches and despite desperate efforts to improve the ground in the short time available they were placed in the second division.

When manager Glyn Watson and several members of the first team were tempted away by big spending Winsford, it became apparent the club would have to start again from scratch next season.

1982-83

The club appointed Frank O Kane as player manager, but only Micky Gardiner of last season's first team regulars remained at the club, as the board cut costs to meet the debts of the previous year's court case. Former players Joe Fleetwood, Gerry Luchka and Fred Wilkinson returned to the Dark Lane and forward Neil Robinson was picked up from Bacup. It was the signing of former goalkeeper Geoff Foster one of the players who had walked out of the club back in 1978 that caused some controversy and saw some members leave the board in disgust.

The season opened with the usual draw but despite Robinson finding the net consistently the clubs form was far from consistent. Gradually O Kane strengthened the squad as former midfielder Peter Cooper returned and last season's players Derek Farnsworth and Ian McCool returned to the fold. An unbeaten run of five games up to December saw the club on the fringe of the promotion race but the club lacked the quality of leading sides Radcliffe Boro and Carnarvon and had to settle for 8th place. The season dragging on till the 20th of May due to another hard winter.

The club bowed out of both senior FA competitions at the first hurdle then beat local rivals Bacup after a replay in the Junior Cup before losing to Leyland in the next round. The inaugural North West counties league Challenge cup proved more to Rossy's liking as Ashton Town, Lytham and three first division sides Formby, Leek and Congleton were all overcome to set up a semi-final with Skelmersdale at Dark Lane unfortunately the home side were well beaten 4-1 on the day to end the clubs cup interest for another season.

1983-84

Manager Frank O Kane brought former players Graham Walton and Ian Nugent back to the club from Darwen and Great Harwood respectively as Rossendale started the season with their customary draw against Salford.

Two wins then saw them challenging at the top of the table before a dreadful second half collapse at home to Droylesden saw them lose 7-3 at Dark Lane. This was followed by two more defeats before O Kane brought in Fred Blackburn from Horwich to resolve the troublesome goalkeeping position. The club then embarked on a run of six consecutive wins that saw them top the table towards the end of October. The wheels then came off in style an 8-3 thrashing by Eastwood Hanley started a run of ten consecutive defeats in all competitions that cost O Kane his job. The club brought in former manager Glyn Watson, who had unsuccessful spells as manager of Winsford and Ashton Utd since leaving Dark Lane. He managed to slow the slide down the table but only two more games were won before the end of the season as the club finished a disappointing 15th just six points clear of the relegation places.

Cup competitions offered little joy, the club did not enter the FA cup due to the costs but did enter the FA vase for the first time beating North Withington 6-2 before crashing out 5-0 to Irlam after having two players sent off. They exited the League Cup at the first hurdle losing 2-1 to third division Vulcan Newton, whilst NPL Marine proved too strong in the Junior Cup turning round a 1-0 half time deficit to win 5-1 at Rossett Park.

Off the field Chairwoman Dorothy Heyworth stepped down at the end of the season to take over the role of Treasurer allowing former player and local businessman Derek Hutchinson to become Chairman. The club also had a main sponsor for the first time as local car dealership J A Taylor took up this role whilst an arrangement with the brewery Tetley's saw a major refurbishment of the Social club take place during the close season.

1984-85

Manager Glyn Watson rang the changes in close season with only Micky Gardiner, Bob Barrass, Wayne Haworth and Peter Lock surviving the close season cull. New signings included Gary Smith from Radcliffe, Neil Callan from Bacup, John Higgins from Haslingden and Dave Eastwood from Nelson whilst former Rossy players Dave O Neill, Mark Capstick and Harry Stevenson returned to Dark Lane.

Amazingly the season opened with win for the first time in ten years, this was followed by two more as Rossy topped the table. Unfortunately, as injuries took their toll the club struggled to maintain their early season form and the club slid down the table. It was a surprise however when the club sacked Watson just before Christmas after a particularly poor performance at home to Padiham.

The club appointed Dave O Neill as player manager early in the New Year and he soon began strengthening the team bringing in striker Paul Beck from Accrington Stanley and handing the number one spot to Steve Hobson. He also brought in forward Mike Miniero and ex Blackburn midfielder Stuart Metcalfe to add experience to the midfield. Results gradually improved and a six match unbeaten run in April ended any threat of relegation as the club finished in 14th position.

The Rossendale team pictured towards the end of the 1984–85 seaso:

Back row: B.Barrass, N. Callan, M.Miniero, S. Hobson, P.Beck, I. Tindall, Steve Connaghan (assistant manager)

Front row: S.Metcalfe, G.Smith, W Haworth, D. O Neill(player manager), M Gardiner and A. Byrom.

1985-86

Manager Dave ONeill's team strengthening had a distinct local flavour as young midfielder Andy Grimshaw signed from Rossendale Amateurs and striker Jimmy Clarke and centre half Neil Yates were signed from Haslingden. Former Blackburn player Paul Round was signed from Chorley and the experienced Mick Higgins returned to the club.

The start to the season was delayed by an hour as the Colwyn Bay coach broke down despite this the Rossy players still knocked off at the usual time allowing a 3-1 lead to slip away for the usual opening day draw to occur. This was followed by two big wins as the forward partnership of Clarke and Beck hit their straps and began to terrorize opposing defences.

A poor October that saw just one point picked up saw Rossy slip off the pace at the top of the table. This was followed by a sixteen match unbeaten run that saw Rossy firmly established as the main rivals of leaders Kirkby Town for the second division title. The clubs met on the 24th of April at Dark Lane and Kirkby won 1-0 to secure the title. Two weeks later a 4-1 win over Atherton LR at Dark Lane ensured promotion for Rossy to the topflight of the NWCFL. Forwards Paul Beck and Jimmy Clarke both topped the thirty goal mark in all competitions, the first time this had happened since Barker and Pearson did it during the 1971–72 season.

Rossy made some progress in the FA competitions falling at the second hurdle in both FA competitions, they lost to NPL Marine after a replay in the Junior Cup or ATS Trophy as it was now known. The club did enjoy a run in the League Cup after needing a replay to overcome Third division Maghull in the first round they defeated Netherfield and Fleetwood of the First division before hammering Lancaster 4-1 in the quarter final to set up a semi final with Warrington. The first leg was lost 2-1 before a cracking cup tie at Dark Lane saw Rossy draw the 2nd leg 3-3 after extra time to bow out 5-4 on aggregate before a gate of 445 the biggest crowd at Dark Lane since the 81-82 season.

With gates increasing markedly and the board attracting major sponsorship from local companies such as J A Taylors and Killelea's the future looked rosy.

The club were rocked at the end of May when manager Dave O Neill resigned after a disagreement with chairman Derek Hutchinson. O Neill was soon snapped up by NWCFL champions Clitheroe as replacement for Eric Whalley who had moved to Accrington Stanley and this sparked an exodus of players as the start to the new season was shrouded in uncertainty.

Rossy squad 1985–86

Back row: Haworth, Gardiner, Connaghan(assistant manager), Walker, Yates, Hobson, Round, Procter, Callan, Chesworth (trainer).

Front row: Grimshaw, Byrom, ONeill, Beck, Miniero, Eastwood.

1986-87

The club promoted assistant manager Steve Connaghan to replace Dave O Neill and he brought in former Rossy favourite Billy Greenan as his assistant. The club had lost Paul Beck, Alan Byrom, Paul

Round and Mick Higgins to Clitheroe and big spending Colne Dynamoes had poached Andy Grimshaw and Jimmy Clarke, so Connaghan faced quite a rebuilding job.

Connaghan used this to give opportunities to fringe players Andy Hornsby, and Dave Mahon and brought in Russell Procter, Andy Darbyshire and Mark Kayley from Haslingden and Simon Holding from Whitworth Valley as well as giving chances to a clutch of local amateur players.

The season opened with a creditable 0-0 draw with Congleton, but the first ten league games yielded just four draws and saw Rossy stuck at the wrong end of the table. The main problem was a lack of goals and Connaghan tried to rectify the problem by giving John Wylie a second chance at this level and bringing in Stuart Lally from Great Harwood. The club were given a boost in November when Jimmy Clarke returned to Dark Lane after his Move to Colne did not work out and Rossy finally won their first league game on the 29th November beating Glossop 4-1.

This was followed by two more wins as the club began to move up the table. The clubs cup exploits and bad weather in January meant the club entered March with twenty league games to play a run of five straight wins saw the club comfortably positioned in mid table before the fixture congestion caught up with them and the last four games were lost to eventually finish in 10th spot.

The FA competitions saw Rossendale best performances for a change, the club reached the third qualifying round of the FA cup beating Colwyn Bay, Bridgenorth after replays and Prescot Cables before losing to Oldbury Utd.

It was the FA Vase that really caught the Rossy public's imagination, Kirkby Town were defeated after a replay before Waterloo Dock were beaten 2-0 in a brutal cup tie. Durham City were then beaten 4-2 after extra time at Dark Lane setting up a Third round tie with Droylesden. Rossy stormed into a 4-0 half time lead only for Droylesden to score three times in the first 20 minutes of the second half, Rossy hung on however to set up a home tie with Tamworth in the fourth round. Heavy snow saw this game postponed before an 88th minute John Wylie goal saw Rossy progress to the fifth round. Rossendale were drawn away to Emley a large Rossy following saw Andy Darbyshire give Rossy the lead before Fielding equalised for Emley, the pivotal moment of the game came on 70 minutes when Emley keeper Ray Dennis pulled off a remarkable double save from a Hornsby free kick and Holding's follow up. The game went to extra time and Emley won the tie thanks to a John Francis goal. Rossy went out of the league cup at the first hurdle and thrashed Fleetwood in Junior Cup before losing to Southport.

Off the field the cup exploits and predominance of local players in the team had seen crowds increase again as the financial position continued to improve enabling the club to clear virtually all old outstanding debts and show a surplus for the first time in years. The formation of a Northern Premier first division saw a massive re-organisation of non-league football in the northwest, however the Rossendale board decided to remain in the NWCFL and earn promotion to the next level.

The 1986–87 squad

Back row: Steve Hobson, Billy Greenan (assistant manager), John Wylie, Phil Crook, Steve Walker, Andy Hornsby, Simon Holding, Neil Yates, Steve Connaghan(manager), Brian Melia(physio).

Front row: Micky Gardiner, Dave Mahon, Alan Livesey, Jimmy Clarke, Wayne Haworth, Russell Procter and Tony Flanagan.

1987-88

The club were boosted by the return to the club of Paul Beck and Paul Round from Clitheroe and Andy Grimshaw from Colne, the club also brought in local lad and former Burnley Starlet Andy Wharton from Colne and Alex Binnie on his release by Blackburn. Also, a reserve side was setup for the first time in years, in an effort to keep the exciting squad of local players together.

The club started the season in blistering form winning 4-0 at Skelmersdale before thrashing Bootle 6-2 in front of a crowd of over 600 at Dark Lane. Rossy won twelve out of an unbeaten thirteen match start to the league season that saw them top the league with only big spending Colne Dynamoes in pursuit.

The club suffered their first defeat at Prescot in November but then embarked on another eight match unbeaten run. Rossendale suffered a second defeat to a controversial last minute penalty at Clitheroe in March and a run of four draws in five games as the prolific forward line of Beck, Clark and Wylie suddenly lost their eye for goal, saw Colne overhaul Rossy.

Another defeat this time at St Helens made FA Vase winners Colne favourites for the title, however as the clubs still had to play each other twice, Rossy still had hope. Rossendale duly beat Colne twice 1-0 in the space of five days in front of a combined attendance of nearly 3000 supporters, but Colne held their nerve to beat Glossop and secure the title on goal difference.

Rossendale made limited progress in Cup competitions Northallerton and Worksop were beaten in the FA Cup before a Ray Hankin inspired Guisborough Town won 3-2 at Dark Lane. In the FA Vase Lancaster City were disposed of before Durham City gained revenge by dumping Rossy out 4-0 at

Ferens Park in the second round. Rossy exited the League Cup in the third round at Warrington after beating Nelson and defeated local rivals Bacup and Daisy Hill in the Junior Cup before being thrashed by Morecambe in the Quarter final. The club also entered the LFA Floodlight league cup winning the group stage before losing at Horwich in the semi-final.

Off the field the clubs finances continued to improve enabling them to restore the floodlights in March as well as undertaking a raft of ground improvements such as re-roofing the main stand and improving the terracing at the Staghills Road end, that would give the club the ground grading to move up to the next level.

1988-89

Prior to the start of the season the only changes saw reserve team manager Gary Warburton take up the Bacup job, this saw several fringe players leave to join Bacup as well as star striker Jimmy Clarke who had become unhappy at sharing the striking duties with with Jocky Wylie and Paul Beck. The only significant addition to the squad was left winger Bob Lancaster from Leyland.

The season started with a disappointing 0-0 draw at Skelmersdale, but the next seven games were won to establish Rossy as one of the leading contenders for the title along with leaders St Helens who had played more games and Knowsley.

Rossy went to the top of the league in December and despite losing Andy Grimshaw to big spending Colne Dynamoes again, they extended their unbeaten start to the season to a club and League record twenty two games. Rossendale lost their first league game at Colwyn Bay on the 18th February, but three wins from the next four games ensured they maintained their lead at the top of the table. The first home league defeat in nearly two years at the hands of Knowsley gave the chasing pack some hope, but when Rossy avoided defeat at closest rivals St Helens at the end of March the title was in the bag. A 1-0 win against St Helens on the 8th of April in front of over 1000 fans secured the title and in true Rossy style the first few bars of Fat bottomed girls blasted from the tannoy at the final whistle before hastily being replaced by the ubiquitous We are the champions.

In the cup competitions the club exited the FA cup in the first qualifying round when an injury and suspension ravaged team lost narrowly at Blyth Spartans, the club also made early exits from the League cup and Junior cup competitions. The FA Vase however was always going to be the clubs main target and Rossy started well with a 6-1 thrashing of Burscough, they then came back from 2-0 down to beat Farsley 3-2 after extra time. Garforth were then beaten to set up a plumb home tie against favourites Emley who had put out holders Colne Dynamoes in the second round. A crowd of 1820 witnessed a cracking cup tie that Rossy deservedly won 3-1. Rossendale were then drawn at home Sudbury in the fifth round and a crowd of 1402 turned up at a rain lashed Dark Lane to see Rossy slither to a narrow 1-0 defeat on a quagmire of a pitch.

Off the field the club continued to invest in the facilities and a prestigious friendly against a strong Manchester United side brought to Dark Lane by Alex Ferguson was watched by over 2000 people and raised a significant amount for the ground development fund. The club were also able to announce a significant four figure shirt sponsorship deal with CRG signs for next season as the club looked forward to a new season in the HFS Loans Northern Premier League first division. Manager Steve Connaghan also picked up the Manager of the year award

Captains Steve Bruce and Micky Gardiner and the two teams pictured before the prestigious friendly with Man Utd.

The successful first team and reserve team squads pictured at the end of the 1988–89 season.

1989-90

Rossendale were disappointed to lose star striker Jocky Wylie to Colne Dynamoes who had now turned full time professional, whilst Andy Wharton decided he did not want to cope with the extra travelling involved and joined Bacup before moving to Torquay later in the year. New signings included local lads Neil Rowbotham and striker Steve Parry both from Accrington Stanley and Clitheroe midfielder Gary Butcher.

The season opened with the usual draw and local rivals Radcliffe were defeated in the first home match. The club then went six games without a win as they adjusted to life in the new league where most sides possessed a top striker and any defensive error was punished by a goal. The club further strengthened the team bringing in left sided player Steve Whitehead from Colne and the with the front two of Beck and Parry building a good understanding the club embarked on a good run up to Christmas culminating in a 2-1 Boxing Day win over league leaders Accrington Stanley in front of over 1200 spectators.

January ended with Rossy handily placed in fifth just behind the leading pack but the loss of keeper Hobson for the rest of the season with a back injury coupled with other injuries and loss of form saw the club win just four of their last seventeen games and slide down the table to finish 13th. The clubs struggles were not helped by a remarkable ten penalty misses over the season from five different penalty takers.

The cup competitions saw Rossy progress to the second qualifying round of the FA cup before losing to cup bogie team Marine, whilst in the FA Vase the club progressed to the fourth round before losing to a Frank Worthington inspired Guiseley. In NPL challenge cup Rossy were unfortunate to be drawn away to Colne Dynamoes in the third round after beating Netherfield and Eastwood, whilst Eastwood gained revenge for their league cup defeat knocking Rossy out of the Division one cup in the second round. Rossy enjoyed their best run in the Junior Cup disposing of Atherton LR before beating Conference side Barrow 4-3 at Dark Lane in a blizzard. This set up a quarter final tie at Dark Lane against high flying Colne Dynamoes and Rossy put up a great show losing narrowly 3-2 after extra time before another large crowd.

At the end of the season manager Steve Connaghan disappointed by the reaction of a section of Rossy fans to the clubs form slump at the end of the season resigned saying he had taken the club as far as he could and wanted a new challenge. The club appointed former Stalybridge Celtic manager Kevan Keelan as his replacement.

1990-91

The collapse of one of the clubs main sponsors prior to the season meant the club had to reorganize the finances and cut back the playing budget and this coupled with the loss of several established players who followed reserve team assistant manager Brent Peters to Glossop meant new manager Kevan Keelan had a far more difficult task than he envisaged when he accepted the post. The job was not made any easier when top striker Paul Beck who had scored forty goals the previous season was tempted away to join his hometown club Accrington Stanley for a fee of £1000.

With only six players who played last season remaining at the club it was not surprising the club made a slow start but with the first fifteen games yielding just two wins and the club languishing in the bottom three the alarm bells were ringing. A three match unbeaten run in October eased the pressure but with Keelan desperately juggling his playing resources in search of a winning formula performances did not improve and when Ossett Town dumped the club out of the Vase at the end of November the manager was axed.

The board promptly brought back Steve Connaghan who had not enjoyed his brief managerial stint at Salford. With the collapse of Colne Dynamoes prior to the season there was a glut of quality players available and Connaghan quickly brought in Duncan McFadyen, Steve Bentley and Carl Parker as well as back room staff, coach Billy Gaskell and the legendary physio Syd Parkinson. With former players Andy Darbyshire and Mark Kayley returning after falling out of favour with previous manager the club began to have a more familiar look. Left back Duncan Edwards arrived from Clitheroe and Haslingden youngsters Lloyd Green and Colin Yeomans also arrived, but the master stroke was the resigning of forward Jocky Wylie from Accrington where he had an unhappy spell after leaving Colne. Not surprisingly results improved immediately and with Wylie scoring goals for fun fourteen in fifteen games the club climbed away from the foot of the table to eventually finish 15th.

Cup competitions offered little joy as the club went out at the first hurdle in both FA competitions to lower league opposition. They also fell at the first hurdle in both NPL cup competitions, they did win one cup game beating Blackpool Mechanics in the Junior cup but lost out to lower league Great Harwood in the next round.

The one bright spot in a difficult season was that gates did hold up the club averaging over 300 for the season to establish themselves as one of the better supported clubs in the division.

1991–92

Manager Steve Connaghan further strengthened the squad bringing former Colne players Simon Westwell and Steve Lampkin. The club were rocked however when both strikers Jocky Wylie and Steve Parry who had routine Knee operations over the summer suffered complications and would both miss the start of the season. In fact, Wylie would never kick a ball in anger again and Parry returned late in the season to play a handful of games before breaking down gain.

The season opened with a 2-0 defeat at Caenarvon but the club bounced back with a win and two draws playing attractive attacking football however the lack of a quality striker meant dominance was not turned into goals and this proved costly as games that should have been won slipped away. With finances tight the manager scoured the loan market for a forward and Mike Carter, Milton Brown and Charlie Bradshaw were all tried without success, the only consistent goalscorer being Ian Pilkington a young striker signed from Whinney Hill. By mid-October Rossy had fourteen points and were just below halfway in the table, but a disastrous run of ten consecutive defeats saw the club slump to the foot of the table by the end of the year.

The club stopped the rot with a 2-2 draw at Lancaster on New Years Day and then followed that up with 1-0 win over Carnarvon at a fog bound Dark Lane. A vital 2-1 win at fellow strugglers Irlam gave the club hope of survival and 5-1 thrashing of Newtown at the end of February lifted the club off the bottom of the table, this result sparked a seven match unbeaten run including crucial wins over Irlam and Alfreton that ensured safety for another season as the club finished 19th.

In the cup competitons the club made early exits in both FA competitions but enjoyed some success in the HFS competitions in the Challenge cup Irlam and Mossley were beaten before Matlock narrowly defeated the club in a replay in the third round. In the Division one cup the club reached the quarter finals before being knocked out by Newtown in a penalty shoot-out after the teams could not be separated after two games. The club also went out of the Junior Cup after extra time in a replay with Horwich RMI.

Off the field Chairman Derek Hutchinson decided to step down and the lack of an obvious replacement saw Steve Connaghan take up the role of chairman as well as manager.

1992-93

Manager Connaghan hoped to have resolved the goal scoring problems of the previous season when he paid a club record £2500 to bring Jimmy Clarke back to Dark Lane from Buxton, along with winger Chris Grimshaw from Accrington Stanley and Barry Diamond from Curzon Ashton. However, the loss of centre half Steve Bentley to a career ending injury along with Tony Flanagan and Mark Kayley to Bacup was to prove more damaging.

The season opened with the usual draw 1-1 at home to Alfreton but this was followed by two defeats and with Clarke's appearances restricted by injury and suspension the club once again found themselves struggling at the wrong end of the table. Things came to a head with a 7-2 thrashing at home to Warrington a disillusioned Steve Connaghan resigned as both Chairman and manager. The club had first Billy Gaskell and then Ian Rishton as caretaker managers as they pondered the managerial appointment. Results did not improve as the winless run was extended to eleven games before the club made Gary Pierce the new boss.

He lost is first game in charge 3-2 at Guiseley despite the heroics of stand in keeper Steve Walker. The new manager brought in defenders Duncan Edwards, Steve Guest and Micky Fuller and the club reeled of four wins on the bounce to move out of the relegation places. Unfortunately, the club also lost star striker Jimmy Clarke who walked out after a row with manager Peirce.

The Christmas period saw heavy defeats by Great Harwood and Farsley Celtic and a further three defeats culminating in a 7-1 defeat at home to Sammy McIlroy's Ashton Utd saw the club part company with Pierce and the Chairman Phil Wynne Daniels and much of the board followed as the financial black hole the club was in became apparent.

Coach Geoff Lutley took over the manager's job but was forced to cut the wage bill and sell his best players as new Chairman Tony Saunders battled to get the club back on a secure footing. Chris Grimshaw was sold to Fleetwood for £500 and Ian Pilkington was sold to Chorley. On the field the clubs winless run continued and when it became apparent relegation was inevitable the club stopped paying expenses completely. Lutley bravely carried on as he struggled to get eleven players to represent the club. The season finished with fifteen consecutive defeats and a record winless run of twenty games as the club finished bottom of the league and faced relegation to the North West Counties league.

1993-94

During the summer the board appointed Brent Peters as manager tempted by his additional talents on the commercial and publicity side as well as his football contacts. With only Steve Walker, Alex Binnie and Micky Fuller remaining from last season's squad Peters tempted back former Rossy favourites, Wayne Howarth, Mark Rawstron, Paul Currie and Duncan McFadyen. Paul Rigby and Stuart Thompson were also signed from Great Harwood and Bacup and the playing budget was stretched further to bring former Burnley players Steve Gardner and Phil Malley whilst the experienced Peter Coyne was signed from Radcliffe and the vastly experienced keeper Barry Siddall was also added to the squad.

The club suffered a first ever defeat against Salford City on the opening day of the season but bounced back with two wins. Results remained inconsistent and the club went into Christmas in ninth place but with games in hand on runaway leaders Atherton LR. Peters brought in experienced ex Wigan and Blackpool defender Colin Methven and forward Darren Emmett from Bury to partner the on loan Burnley striker Brian Welch and the club embarked on a run of seven wins to establish themselves in the top three. This was extended to an unbeaten run of ten games before a surprise defeat at Penrith. The club then went on a seven game unbeaten run to establish themselves in second place but a defeat at Bradford PA ended any hopes they had of catching leaders Atherton LR and the club eventually finished four points behind the champions.

The club made limited progress in the FA competitions falling at the second hurdle and the ATS Junior Cup and Floodlit Cup also saw early exits. The NWCFL Challenge cup was a different matter League leaders Atherton were comfortably beaten 3-0 in the first round before the club survived scare at Nelson before winning the replay 4 -1. Maine Road were beaten 1-0 in a bad tempered Quarter Final before second division Stantondale were easily beaten 6-0 on aggregate in the semis to set up a final against St Helens at Gigg Lane. The final was a dour affair with Rossy winning their first Cup final for twenty years 1-0 thanks to a scrambled Darren Emmett goal.

Off the field despite enjoying their most successful season for five years income had failed to meet expenditure and the clubs poor financial position meant the board could not agree a budget for the new season with manager Brent Peters who wanted to take control of the club and had to part company a few weeks before the new season.

The successful 1993–94 squad pictured at the start of the season.

Back row left to right: R McDowell, D Emmott, S Gardner, P Coyne, N Yates, A Binnie, S Yates, C Greenwood, P Guest.

Middle row: S Holding (assistant manager), P Whittaker, D McFadyen, K Grimshaw, C Nash, B Siddall, R Bridges, S Walker, M Hussain, P Malley, S Parkinson(physio).

Front row: S Thompson, P Rigby, M Rawstron, B Peters(manager), W Haworth, S Pearson, T Kershaw.

The successful Rossy team with the North West Counties League Cup.

Back row: Paul Currie, Paul Rigby, Colin Little, Barry Siddall, Colin Methven, Billy Haworth(kit man), Mark Rawstron, Andy Jones, Brian Welch and Steve Gardner.

Front row: Syd Parkinson(physio), Darren Emmett, Duncan McFadyen, Peter Coyne, Brent Peters(manager), Simon Holding(assistant manager) and Phil Malley.

1994-95

Former Flixton manager Chris Nicholson was given the manager's job just prior to the season with just goalkeeper Carlo Nash and club stalwart Steve Walker remaining from the previous season. He did a remarkable job in getting a squad together that won two and drew two of the first four games the clubs best start to a season since 1988–89. Much of the success was built on the goalscoring exploits of Lee Scriggins and the midfield guile of former Man Utd trainee and Eire U21 international Kieran Toal.

The club were handily placed in the top eight at the end of October, but just one more league game was won before Christmas when Scriggins emigrated to Australia where he had played for Brisbane previously. The winless run was extended to eleven games and with Rossy being dragged down the table Nicholson resigned at the end of February. Gerry Keenan who had been helping with the coaching took over as manager until the end of the season and result improved as the club finished 18th well clear of the bottom two.

The Club defeated Ossett Albion to earn a home tie with Matlock that was narrowly lost in the FA Cup, but the club suffered first round exits in all other competitions apart from the ATS Junior cup where Nelson were overcome setting up a home tie with Conference side Southport who won easily but were expelled from the competition for playing an ineligible player. This earned Rossy a trip to another Conference side Morecambe who won 5-0.

Off the field crowds stood up well but the financial position was still perilous, and the club consistently lost players to clubs playing higher wages making the manager's job even harder.

1995–96

Gerry Keenan was forced to step down over the summer due to family and work commitments and with no money in the kitty to attract any quality managerial candidates the club made Scott Moore player manager. The club had already seen its best players such as Carlo Nash leave, but Scott worked hard to get a squad together to start the season and once again the first game was drawn. Rossy then defeated Salford but reality soon struck as the next eight games were lost with thirty one goals conceded and just one scored.

The rot was stopped with a draw with Eastwood Hanley, this was followed by a vital win over bottom club Skelmersdale and a shock win at title chasing Trafford. Normal service was soon resumed and after two consecutive 7-0 defeats at St Helens and Eastwood Hanley the club parted company with Scott in December.

The new manager was former Darwen reserve team boss Gary Blackshaw, who brought Micky Graham to the club as his assistant. Rossy managed a win over fellow strugglers Salford but just two more game were won as the club finished next to bottom but avoided relegation thanks to league reorganisation.

The cup offered little respite Blidworth were overcome after a replay in the FA Cup but Colwyn Bay put an end to that run with a 4-1 win at Dark Lane every other cup game was lost including an embarrassing 9-0 defeat at Brigg in the FA Vase.

Off the pitch new chairman Jack Feber and a small band of volunteers worked hard to keep the club afloat, but with the ground looking increasingly dilapidated it was clear that any spare money available would have to be spent bringing facilities up to scratch and not on the playing side.

1996–97

The club once again started the season with a new manager with Micky Graham taking over from Gary Blackshaw and he appointed the experienced John Hughes as his player assistant manager.

The season opened with a defeat at fancied Newcastle Town and the first four games brought just one point, the club did manger their first win at Blackpool Rovers but this was followed by five defeats that saw the club languishing at the foot of the table. Then vital wins over fellow strugglers Holker OB and Chadderton lifted Rossy off the foot of the table.

The management continued to strengthen the squad bringing in centre backs Mick Bennett and Darren Zoldan and forwards Danny Heys and Darren Maloney but could not string a winning run together with mixed results like a 2-0 win at title chasing Mossley followed by a 4-1 home drubbing by fellow strugglers Glossop. A strong finish that saw four wins and two draws from the last nine games ensured safety for Rossy as they eventually finished seventeenth, five points clear of the bottom two.

The FA cup saw Rossy defeat Castleton Gabriels after a replay to set up a lucrative home game with Conference side Southport and a crowd of over 500 witnessed a closer tie than the 5-0 scoreline to the visitors suggests. The only other cup victory was also over Castleton in the Floodlight Trophy as the club exited the other cup competitions at the first opportunity.

Off the field a storm in February wrecked the perimeter fencing opposite the grandstand to drain finances further but the club did complete work on upgrading the dressing rooms to maintain the clubs ground grading. Both Micky Graham and John Hughes were keen on youth development and the club developed links with local Junior setups that saw the establishment of a Youth team for the following season.

The Rossy team pictured at the start of the 1996–97 season.

Back row: Mark Heys, Damien McKay, Mark Hodgson, Neil Perry, Paul Horridge, Paul Smith, Jamie Smith, Steve Pickup, Paul Holdsworth:

Front Row: Scott McQuarrie, Peter Shaw, John Hughes (assistant manager), Micky Graham(manager), Martin Pearce Billy Howcroft

1997-98

With much of last season's squad remaining manager Micky Graham brought in striker Paul Thomson from Tottington and Matty Knowles from Eagley, whilst keeper Paul Horridge was brought back to replace Lee Greenacre who had been signed by Bamber Bridge. The club also started a reserve side again to provide progression for the youth team players.

The season opened with defeat at promotion favourites Newcastle Town and the first seven games brought just one win as the team found themselves in the relegation places. Three wins at the end of September boosted the club up table and with forwards Thomson and Maloney scoring regularly the club continued to climb the table in an erratic win three lose three fashion.

Despite having to cut players expenses the team stayed loyal and four wins in five games at the end of March saw the club reach a high point of 8th before a tired run in of one point from the last eight games saw the club finish in 13th position.

In the FA Cup Blidworth Welfare were beaten 5-3 before a classy Ilkeston team proved too good in the next round. The club made progress in the FA Vase for the first time in several years beating Worsborough Bridge and East Manchester before losing 2-1 in a tight game with eventual finalists Tow Law in the second round. The club made no progress in the other cup competitions a 1-0 extra time defeat to local rivals Bacup in the Junior cup proving particularly galling.

Off the field ground improvements continued to take priority leaving little money for the playing side. Plans were in full swing to celebrate the clubs centenary starting with a centenary dinner that was well attended by former players and raised vital funds for the club.

1998-99

During the summer the club continued to make improvements to the ground with a new perimeter fence on the far side and Staghills Road end of the ground and new concrete walkways. On the field the club had lost leading scorer Paul Thomson to Ramsbottom, whilst the demise of Haslingden had seen the signing of John Richardson and the return of Steve Pickup, whilst promising young player Jerome Fitzgerald was signed from Darwen.

The season started slowly with just one win from the first seven league games which saw the club in 17th position and struggling for goals. The introduction of 17 year old youth team player Craig Sargeson solved that problem as he scored five goals in his first six games four of which were won moving the club up to mid table.

The management team continued to give youth a chance throughout the season and consequently struggled for consistency and a run of five defeats towards the end of the year saw the club slide back down the table. Micky Graham brought in Shaun Bursnell, Simon O Brien and Jason Heffernan to add a bit of experience and a run of four wins from five games towards the end of March ensured a comfortable mid table finish. With the young tyro Sargeson netting 22 goals on his debut season and youngsters like schoolboy Vinny Pattison impressing when given a run towards the end of the season, things on the field seemed to be on the up.

There was limited progress in the cup competitions Brigg proved too strong in the FA Cup and East Manchester were once again beaten in the Vase before a disappointing exit at Liversedge in the first round. There was little or no progress in the League cup or Junior Cups but the club enjoyed a run in the Floodlit Trophy beating Castleton Gabriels and St Helens , the St Helens result being particularly impressive as six members of the youth team were involved in the win over a strong St Helens team. This set up a quarter final with Darwen which was comfortably won 3-1 only for the club to be expelled when it became apparent that Shaun Bursnell was ineligible having played for Clitheroe earlier in the competition.

Off the field Boxing Day storms wrecked the turnstile block and brought down large sections of the new fencing placing another financial burden on the club who ended their centenary season not knowing if it would be their last. As it was not long after the season ended local businessman Andrew Connolly bought the club paying off an estimated historical debt of £34,000 and along with his wife Sandra taking over the running of the club.

The players of Rossy and Man City pictured before a friendly prior to the 1999–2000 season.

1999-00

The new season began with a renewed optimism, new owner Andrew Connolly had invested heavily in improving the ground and over the course of the season was to upgrade the Floodlights, provide covered standing at both ends improve the tea hut and social club.

On the pitch manager Micky Graham with money to spend for the first time strengthened the squad. He brought in experience in local lads Andy Grimshaw and Jim McLuskie and former Burnley midfielder John Borland all from Accrington Stanley and preseason wins over Sheffield Utd and a strong Wigan Athletic team augured well for the new season.

As usual the season started with a draw 1-1 at Prescot but Rossy extended an unbeaten start to four league games before Clitheroe inflicted the first defeat of the season. Manager Micky Graham continued to introduce new players with Ged Walsh returning after eight years. Matt Houldsworth and Neil Ollerton were also added to improve the quality of the squad, but consistency remained elusive even within the same game. However, as the team settled down an unbeaten run of seven games saw the team climb to 6th twelve points behind leaders Vauxhall Motors but with four games in hand. The signings of keeper Mark Andrews from Chorley and Steve Cunningham from Atherton LR helped Rossy keep progressing, but they had too much to do to catch leaders Vauxhall, although they were in with a chance of runners up spot until the last day of the season when a draw saw the club finish a highly creditable 5th.

Once again, the start performer was teenage goalscoring sensation Craig Sargeson who bagged 39 goals in his second season.

With high hopes for the season the FA competitions were disappointing, after beating Chadderton and missing a host of chances in the first game the club bowed out to Ossett Town in a replay in the FA Cup.

Even worse was to follow in the Vase as Rossy fell at the first hurdle beaten 3-2 after extra time by Curzon Ashton whilst Skelmersdale pulled of a rare win to knock Rossy out of the League cup in the second round. The club enjoyed more success in the Marsden Junior Cup reaching the Quarter finals before losing 3-2 at conference side Barrow.

It was the Floodlit Trophy that brought most success as Ramsbottom and St Helens were overcome after replays before Mossley and Salford were defeated to set up a final at Dark Lane against Champions elect Vauxhall Motors. A crowd of over 500 witnessed a cracking game that saw Danny Heys give Rossy a second half lead, Vauxhall equalised late in the game from a corner and proved too strong in extra time to run out 3-1 winners.

With Micky Graham building a useful side and the work at the ground already gaining a NPL grading the pressure would be on next season to win promotion.

2000-01

The main signings prior to the season saw Darren Norman and Dave Gray return to the club from Clitheroe and Northwich, combative midfielder Paul Lynch sign from Darwen and striker Andy Gayle from Nantwich.

The season opened with a rare opening day win at fancied Newcastle Town, but this was followed by home defeats by Clitheroe and Nantwich. Many in the local football community were shocked when owner Andrew Connolly reacted to the poor start by sacking Micky Graham and appointing Jim McLuskie as the new manager. McLuskie's reign did not get off to the best of starts as the club exited the FA Cup and then lost a third league game at Salford.

McLuskie soon put his stamp on the team bringing in centre half's Gary Rishton from Clitheroe and Steve Bird from Bangor City, moving Matt Houldsworth to right back and bringing in Jerome Fitzgerald to the left wing. Results improved as Craig Sargeson found his shooting boots and a ten match unbeaten run saw the club end the year in eleventh place after a Boxing day defeat at Ramsbottom.

Cup replays and postponements in one of the wettest winters in memory meant the club had plenty of games in hand to catch the leaders. Rossy started the year with vital wins at fellow championship chasers Clitheroe and Prescot as they began a fourteen match unbeaten run that saw the club climb to the top of the table scoring 48 goals and conceding just 12. During this run McLuskie had further strengthened the side bringing experienced forward Paul Heavey, winger Gareth Gardiner and midfielder Gareth Webster as the games came thick and fast. Having got to the top of the table Rossy promptly lost at Skelmersdale giving up top spot to Clitheroe. McLuskie then brought in the mercurial forward Jody Banim from Hyde for the run in and the club bounced back with four wins including vital ones against Newcastle Town and Fleetwood Freeport that ended their challenges at the top.

Easter arrived with Rossy top of the league and clear favourites but the wheels came off as they lost to title challengers St Helens home and away and close rivals Ramsbottom in the space of four days. The Ramsbottom defeat was particularly hard to take as it was watched by the biggest gate for years 702 and a Ramsbottom side reduced to ten men out fought and out thought a tired looking Rossy team to win 1-0. Wins over Maine Road, Mossley and Glossop saw Rossy return to the top of the table as the teams around them all took points off each other. A terrific 4-2 win over Kidsgrove at Dark Lane took the visitors out of the reckoning and if results went for them a last day victory at Flixton would clinch the title and promotion to the Northern Premier League. Rossy duly won 4-0 at Flixton in front of 400 travelling Rossy fans and when news came through that Clitheroe and St Helens had drawn 0-0 the celebrations began.

Rossendale suffered an early exit in the FA Cup losing to Sheffield 2-1 the game being played at Bramall Lane as the hosts new ground was not ready. The club enjoyed some success in the Vase beating Chadderton, Parkgate and Selby before losing 3-2 at home to Brigg when some controversial refereeing decisions saw Rossy reduced to nine men. The club made little impact in other competitions losing to Leigh in the Junior cup after beating Atherton Colls 6-4 in the first round and being expelled from the league cup after beating Padiham 2-0 after playing an ineligible player.

Rossy enjoyed a great league season scoring over a 100 league goals for the first time in nearly forty years with Craig Sargeson finishing the league top scorer with 39 goals in all competitions, this saw him reach a 100 goals for the club in just 148 games and all this before his 21st birthday. Over 4500 fans passed through the turnstiles for league games at an average of 233 making Rossy the best supported club in the league and optimism was high that the club would find no problem in adjusting to football at a higher level.

The Rossendale squad pictured with the North West Counties Championship Trophy.

2001-02

The club strengthened the squad with the signings of Darren Bowman and Chris Wilcox from Ramsbottom and the vastly experienced former Blackburn, Bury and Sheffield Utd midfielder Mark Patterson from Accrington Stanley. They replaced the likes of Paul Heavey and who decided not to make the step up to Unibond League football due to the extra travel. The club also lost star striker Jody Banim to local rivals Radcliffe just prior to the season after a disagreement with the management.

The season opened with a rare opening day victory at Matlock and it was September before a solid Rossy defence conceded a goal as they established themselves at the top of the table before suffering their first defeat of the season at the hands of big spending Harrogate Town at the end of September. Injuries to key players Mark Andrews and Steve Bird and the departure of Mark Patterson who took the Assistant managers job at Scarborough saw Rossy's form dip as they slipped down to ninth by the end of November.

Manager Jim McLuskie brought in Ricky Harris from Leigh RMI and former Burnley defender Chris Scott and he was rewarded as four wins saw the club climb to fourth by the turn of the year earning McLuskie the manager of the month award for December. Rossy found goals hard to come by in the new year until the loan signing of striker Gary Williams from Accrington Stanley saw run of four wins in five games in April that kept the clubs play-off hopes alive but the season finished with three defeats and the club had to be content with a creditable ninth place in their first season back in the Unibond league.

Rossy enjoyed some success in the FA Cup beating Garforth, Guisborough and Thackley to set up a third qualifying tie at Barrow where a superb display from reserve team keeper Billy Carrington earned a replay. A crowd of over 1000 turned up for the replay and saw a cracking game end 3-3 after extra time but Barrow came out on top in the penalty shoot-out, crucially for the club Steve Bird suffered a broken leg in this game that both the player and the club never really recovered from. The League cup was played on a group basis and this saw the clubs last competitive meeting with Accrington Stanley as the competition was used to give fringe players some football. In the Lancashire Junior Cup Flixton were beaten before Leigh RMI won 4-3 in the next round.

Overall the season was judged a success with gates averaging around 250 hopes were high the club could make an assault on promotion next season.

2002-03

Off the field improvements to the ground continued with a new set of floodlights and a brand new playing surface. On the playing side Assistant manager Andy Grimshaw moved to Ramsbottom to extend his playing career and St Helens manager Jim McBride was brought in as the new assistant and he was instrumental in bringing forward Gary Jensen from Prescot and defenders Chris Fitzsimmons from Abersystwyth and Matt Woods from Chester. The club also paid a record transfer fee to bring striker Gary Williams to the club on a permanent basis from Accrington Stanley.

The season started in disappointing fashion with defeats at Chorley and Ossett before a five match unbeaten run started moving Rossy up the table. The club were rocked when influential midfielder Paul Lynch suffered a career ending broken leg at Eastwood Town and picked up only one point from the next six games as the club slid down the table. The rot was stopped by a win over Kidsgrove but heavy defeats followed at the hands of Stocksbridge and Kendal, despite this the club was shocked when manager Jim McLuskie resigned at the beginning of November after a 3-1 win over Bishop Auckland.

Jim McBride was promoted to manager and his reign started with four league defeats that threatened the club with a relegation fight. McBride acted swiftly to stop the rot bringing goalkeeper John Gillies from Marine to replace the injured Mark Andrews and former Chesterfield midfielder Chris Perkins as well as the experienced Dave Gamble from Southport. Results improved although consistency was rarely established as forty four players were used during the season. However, the club moved into a comfortable mid table position before a run of five defeats in the last six games saw them finish in 18th position.

The club bowed out at the first time of asking in the FA competitions but enjoyed some success in the Lancashire Trophy beating Colne and enjoying a very rare cup win over Marine before losing to Leigh RMI in the quarter finals. It was in the NPL Challenge cup that the club enjoyed most success beating Premier division Droylesden, Lancaster City and Vauxhall Motors as well as Workington to reach the semi-finals where another Premier division team Gateshead proved too strong winning 4-0 at the International stadium.

2003-04

Off the field owner Andrew Connolly stepped back from the day to day running of the club appointing local businessmen Steve Draper as Chairman and Declan Callan as vice chairman. On the field manager Jim McBride brought in goalkeeper Matt Taylor from FA Vase winners Burscough, Karl Bell and Lee Badrock from St Helens, full back Dave Swannick from Morecambe and forward Doni Clarke from Huddersfield in attempt to secure a twelfth place finish that would guarantee premier division football after reorganisation due to the introduction of Conference North and South in 2004.

The season opened with a narrow 1-0 defeat at Farsley followed by two home wins, but a winless run of five games in the league saw the new board panic and dismiss McBride despite still being in the FA Cup. Former player Paul Lynch was appointed manager and this saw an influx of former players such as Steve Bird, Steve Cunningham and Mark Andrews as well as an ill-fated flirtation with Clitheroe players Neil Reynolds, Chris Whittingham and Lee Cryer. The improvement to results was marginal and Jim McLuskie was tempted back initially as consultant but soon took over as manager until the end of the season as Rossy threw significant amounts of money at achieving that top twelve finish, as players such as Simon Burton Greg Challender and Brian Welch were brought in. The team failed to put together a good run of results but as the season came to a close the reorganisation meant a 14th place would be enough for promotion and as it turned out a win against Belper would have secured this, unfortunately the season ended with a 0-0 draw and 15th place finish one point behind Leek Town.

The FA Cup saw Rossy beat Goole and Harrogate Railway to progress to the second qualifying round but the ill-timed sacking of Jim McBride saw a makeshift team go down 3-1 at Marine. In the FA Trophy Colwyn Bay and Bridlington were beaten, then Rossy were beaten by Guiseley after a replay. The NPL competitions brought little joy as Rossy exited the challenge cup in the second round losing heavily at Vauxhall Motors whilst Bridlington gained revenge for their FA Trophy defeat dumping Rossy out of the Presidents Cup in the first round. The season closed with a Charity game with a useful Man Utd side in memory of club stalwart David Taylor who was tragically killed in Rawtenstall earlier in the year.

2004-05

New Chairman Declan Callan had to dramatically scale back the playing budget for the new management team of Ashley Hoskin and Hughie Bridge and only four players remained from the previous season, Chris Brooks, Phil Lockett, Ian Barker and Jordan Rispin. The new management team brought in keeper Paul Eatock from Chorley but the rest of the squad had very little experience at Unibond level and despite creditable draws away at Willenhall and Telford a run of three consecutive five goal defeats and an embarrassing 4-1 defeat at home to Liversedge in the FA cup saw the club sack Hoskin before the end of September.

The club acted swiftly bringing in former Chorley manager Mark Molyneux as player manager. Molyneux brought in the experienced Wayne Goodison as his assistant and a host of players such as Stuart Tulloch, Dean Cooper, Jamie Baguley, Rob Jones and Paul Varley who had been with Molyneaux at his previous clubs. Not surprisingly it took a few games for things to improve, the first win of the season arriving in the eleventh game a 2-1 win over Kidsgrove. A four match unbeaten run in November lifted the club off the bottom of the table and raised hopes of survival but this was followed by four more defeats before a crucial 3-0 win at fellow strugglers Chorley gave the club hope. The club earned enough wins to move clear of bottom club Rocester but constant changes to the team fifty one players were used over the season meant the club failed to move out of the bottom two. However, the demotion of Spennymoor to the Northern League ensured the club avoided relegation.

The Cup competitons saw the club fail to progress on any front the nearest the club came to success was a defeat to Woodley 6-5 on penalties in the Chairman's cup. Off the field despite another fall in gates the club had managed to stabilise the financial position and there was hope progress could be made next season.

2005-06

The highlight of pre-season was the visit of a Manchester Utd reserve side that contained Roy Keane after his fall out with Alex Ferguson and brought the Sky Sports News cameras to Dark Lane, a strong Utd side won 7-0 but not before Rossy had a penalty saved by new Utd keeper Ben Foster just before half time with score at 0-0.

The season proper opened promisingly with two draws and a win but the club failed to gain a win in the next seven games as they slid down the table. The club stopped the rot with back to back wins over fellow strugglers Belper and Kendal but manager Mark Molyneux's constant tinkering had failed solve Rossy's defensive frailties and it was no surprise when he was sacked at the beginning of November after former Rossy legend Steve Hobson had taken over as Chairman. The club brought in Ramsbottom manager Derek Egan as his replacement and he built a new team bringing back former Rossy favourites Mark Andrews and Matt Raywood along with Billy Robertson , Bernard Morley, and Matt Edgington all from Ramsbottom. The new manager had an instant impact as the club embarked on a run of just one defeat in eighteen games lifting the club to the edge of the play offs. The new manager continued to strengthen the team as defender Russell Clarke was brought in from Clitheroe along with Joe Booth, Kyle Ingham and Neil Zarac a forward from Chorley who bagged fourteen goals in nineteen games during this run. Unfortunately, key midfielder Morley broke his leg and Centre half Clarke also suffered a bad injury as the season finished with a run of five defeats as the club eventually finished fifteenth.

The FA Cup saw the club reach the 3rd qualifying round for the first time in 4 years defeating Northern league Billingham Town and Sunderland Nissan after replays and Armthorpe Welfare before losing narrowly to 1-0 at home to Blyth Spartans. The club made no impact in any other competition failing at the first hurdle in all of them.

Off the field optimism was high as the club announced a link up with local company Sponsorbank which Chairman Steve Hobson hoped would secure the clubs financial security.

2006-07

Manager Derek Egan continued to strengthen the side bringing in defenders Danny Warrender from Blackpool and Dean Whittal-Williams from Colwyn Bay midfielder Phil Edgehill from Curzon Ashton and former Burnley and Morecambe forward Phil Eastwood from Stalybridge.

The season started slowly with only two points from the first four games, but a run of eight wins in eleven games lifted Rossy up into play-off contention, but the loss of keeper Salisbury to a career ending shoulder injury meant the keeper position was then filled by five different players and this linked with the loss of captain and centre half Bill Robertson who took up a professional contract in Australia saw Rossy gradually slide down the table after the Christmas period winning just one of eleven games in the new year.

A strong finish that saw Rossy win six of their last nine games saw the club move up the table to finish ninth a frustrating seven point off a play-off place.

The cup competitions brought little comfort Consett were overcome in the FA cup after a replay before another trip to the North East saw Rossy beaten convincingly by Gateshead. Rossy reached the quarter finals of the Lancashire trophy beating Blackpool Mechanics on penalties the only penalty success in the club's history and Nelson before losing 3-0 at Marine. In the UniBond league competitons the club fell at the first hurdle losing to Skelmersdale in the League cup and at Ashton Utd in the Chairmans Cup.

Off the field the link up with Sponsorbank was not proving as fruitful as the club hoped and with crowds flatlining and owner Andrew Connolly putting the club up for sale the financial situation was still a worry for club officials.

2007-08

With the second tier of the Northern Premier League split into a North and a South section Rossendale kept most of last season's squad together, the main signing being experienced keeper Lee Bracey.

The season opened promisingly with two wins and a draw before promotion favourites FC United of Manchester visited Dark Lane, Rossy lost a tight game 2-1 before a crowd of 2023 the biggest for a competitive game at Dark Lane since the visit of Shrewsbury in the FA Cup thirty two years ago. A slump in form followed which saw just one win in eight games including a 9-0 drubbing at Bradford PA. A 4-1 win over Skelmersdale was then followed by five defeats as the club slumped dangerously close to the relegation zone. A seven match unbeaten run in December lifted the club up the table, as experienced players Andy Watson and Mario Daniel were added to the squad. The team finished the season strongly and a 4-2 win over champions Bradford PA on the last day of the season saw the club finish in ninth fifteen points off a play-off place. A hat-trick from Phil Eastwood saw him top the twenty goal mark for the season the first player to achieve this since Craig Sargeson five years previously.

The FA Cup saw Rossy crash out at the first attempt with an embarrassing defeat at home to lowly Dinnington Town, whilst they also fell at the first hurdle in the FA trophy losing 3-2 at Warrington, who also dumped them out of League cup. Local rivals Clitheroe were beaten in the President cup setting up a lucrative tie at FC United which was lost narrowly 2-1. In the Lancashire Cup Skelmersdale were seen off before a narrow 3-2 defeat at Conference side Southport ended Rossy's cup hopes for another season.

Overall boosted by the FC united and Bradford games gates were well up on the previous season and with the club's main sponsor Killeleas continuing to back the club Chairman Steve Hobson was hopeful of mounting a promotion push the following season.

2008-09

The close season saw the club invest in some extensive drainage work on the pitch which looked in excellent condition as the season opened. On the field the club were sad to see midfield star Joe Booth depart to his local side AFC Fylde for family reasons, but were boosted when former skipper Bill Robertson signed on until his return to Australia in October. Other signings saw local forward Micky Saunders join from Fleetwood, Craig Flowers from Stockport and Marcus Calvert from Crewe.

Despite a heavy 5-0 opening day defeat at one of the promotion favourites Newcastle Blue Star a run of two wins and two draws and progress in the FA cup meant the club had made a reasonable start to the season. A return of one point from the next five league games as well as heavy defeats in both FA competitions heaped pressure on manager Derek Egan who resigned at the end of October.

The club appointed star forward Phil Eastwood as caretaker manager. Victory over league leaders FC Halifax secured Phil the job until the end of the season and Rossy secured a double over FC Halifax and ended the year with a win at Radcliffe that saw Rossy well clear of bottom club Salford. However, a run of just three points from the next ten games coupled with big spending Salford's revival set alarm bell ringing. When Salford did the double over Rossy in the space of three weeks towards the end of the season it became a two horse race for survival. Rossy entered the last game at home to Mossley knowing only a win would guarantee survival and promptly went 3-0 down in the first nine minutes, a missed penalty midway through the first half effectively ended any Rossy chances of a comeback and a Salford win at Garforth condemned Rossy to a bottom place finish.

Rossy enjoyed limited success in the FA Cup beating Oldham Boro after a replay and Woodley Sports before being outclassed by Durham in the second Qualifying round. The FA Trophy proved a disaster as Rossy were thrashed 8-1 at Trafford, it was a result that probably sealed manager Egan's fate as he spent half time arguing with Rossy supporters who were unhappy at being 5-0 down rather than in the dressing room trying to lift his players. The club also made first round exits in the league cup and Presidents cup at the hand of Woodley sports and Bamber Bridge respectively. There was some joy in the Lancashire Trophy as local rivals Clitheroe were beaten 2-1 before Southport knocked Rossy out beating them 3-1 at Dark Lane.

Rossendale were given a reprieve at the FA meeting in June when the usual promotion shenanigans to level four saw Rossy avoid relegation as they had the second best record of the bottom placed clubs. It came too late for manager Phil Eastwood who had resigned to continue his playing career at Bamber Bridge and most of the better players had left the club to secure UniBond level football elsewhere.

2009-10

Rossy Chairman Steve Hobson appointed John Hughes as Manager, John was no stranger to the club having spent five years at the club as both a player and Assistant manager in the late 1990's. With only three players remaining from the previous season the manager had a big task to build a team for the coming season. Amongst a host of signings those of former England youth international goalkeeper Tom Brocklehurst from Bolton, the return of Sean Pearson to the club, Keith Wedge from Abbey Hey and a youngster from Blackburn Jason Hart stood out.

The season opened with a 3-1 defeat at home to Leigh Genesis and after a return of one point from the first four games the writing was already on the wall. A hard earned victory over Prescot coupled with progress in the FA Cup raised hopes, but the next league victory did not come until December by which time Rossy were stuck in the bottom two and a fierce relegation battle.

The manager had already used over forty players by this stage in the search for an effective combination but apart from the impressive Brocklehurst in goal none had shown the consistency or class to suggest the club could avoid the drop this year. With the club bottom going into March they invested in a last ditch survival bid bringing in loanees Ryan Zico Black from Lancaster, Dan Shannon from Workington and Nick Swirad from FC United. This paid dividend as a five match unbeaten run starting with 3-1 win over league leaders Curzon Ashton brought them in touch with Ossett Albion, but the recall of Shannon by Workington and limp home defeats against struggling Harrogate Railway and Garforth condemned the club to relegation to the North West Counties League.

In the FA Cup Rossy overcame Trafford in a replay before bowing out 4-1 at AFC Fylde in the 1st qualifying round. Local rivals Chorley knocked Rossy out of the FA Trophy winning 2-1 in a tight game at Dark Lane. In the League Cup local rivals Clitheroe were once again put to the sword at Dark Lane for the third year in a row but Curzon Ashton won comfortably in the second round, whilst Skelmersdale beat Rossy 3-0 in the Presidents Cup. The Lancashire trophy saw Rossy record their biggest win of the season beating Squires Gate 4-1 before losing narrowly 3-2 at Conference side Barrow in the next round.

Off the field the poor season had seen gates slump with ten games failing to attract three figure crowds, although a gate of 745 for the visit of FC Halifax boosted the average attendance. This obviously affected club finances and with the owner still looking to sell the club and unwilling to pump any of his own money in the board were under pressure to keep finances in check.

Back Row Left to Right: Papis Dieyte, Jack Brierley, Robert Flint, Tom Smith, Tom Brocklehurst, Chris Lawton, Andrew Charlesworth, Paul Socha, Kanganl Ndiwa.

Front Row Left to Right: Demaine Cousins, Matt Walsh, Sean Pearson, Jason Hart, Danny Ellis, Danny Finch, Alex Leke.

2010-11

Most fans were hopeful that a spell in the North West Counties with plenty of local derbies and less travelling would give the club an opportunity to stabilize and the club kept faith with manager John Hughes hoping he would keep the club at the top end of the table, with the majority of the previous seasons squad staying with the club.

The season opened with two defeats but with young forwards Danny Doherty and Jason Hart both finding the net the club embarked on a six match unbeaten run and this coupled with progress in the FA Cup meant things were looking up. Unfortunately, the loss of keeper Brocklehurst as he needed an operation on his back and Jason Hart to suspension saw form dip. At the same time the relationship between Chairman Steve Hobson and the owner Andrew Connolly went into terminal decline when Connolly hit the board with unpaid tax bills of over £20,000. The club cut all wages and when the club exited the FA Vase in October the Manager John Hughes left the club.

Coaches Paul Colgan and Gary Brown took over the management and despite the lack of funds persuaded most of the players to stay loyal to the club. The club then lost the next eight league games and slumped to the foot of the table before the slump was stopped with 1-1 draw with Squires Gate on the 20th November. This proved to be the last game of 2010 as the big freeze set in. At the beginning of December the relationship between the board and owner Andrew Connolly completely broke down and the board resigned en masse on the 12th of December. The management team of Paul Colgan and Gary Brown agreed to stay on and ran the club with the help of a small team of volunteers as Andrew Connolly vowed to keep the club going until the end of the season.

Although performances did improve Rossy's winless run stretched to seventeen games as the number of players used topped the sixty mark. The club finally seemed to hit the buffers on the 22nd of February when with the owner away in Spain the water was cut off forcing the postponement of the home game with Runcorn Linnets. This proved the final straw for hardworking manager Colgan who resigned. With the club in turmoil the league cancelled the next two games and gave the club an ultimatum to complete the fixture at home to Winsford on the 5th of March or be kicked out of the league. This led to a spate of vandalism and social club was broken into and vandalised to such an extent that it was unusable closing one more stream of revenue.

A small number of volunteers from the Supporters Association rallied round and with Connolly agreeing to carry on until the end of the season it was game on. All that was needed was a team and former players Chris Brooks and Jamie Baguley agreed to take on the management role and raise a team. Ironically, despite the lack of cash the players brought in mainly fringe players from a higher level such as Steve Burke and Grant Spencer, the quality of football improved dramatically and although result were inconsistent due to the difficulty in turning out a regular eleven, the club improved enough to finish well above bottom club Ashton Athletic winning the last game of the season against Maine Road 1-0.

The FA Cup had opened with much promise as Formby and Cammell Laird were well beaten bringing in much needed funds before the club lost out by the odd goal in seven against Leigh Genesis. The club bowed out at the first attempt in all other competitions including that second round FA Vase defeat against local rivals Bacup Borough.

The season ended in uncertainty as emergency meetings were held and owner Connolly revealed the extent of the debts of over £60,000 including the £24,000 owed to the tax man and made it clear he was unwilling to continue. With nobody prepared to take on the club and with charges against the ground meaning Connolly could not sell it at an affordable price the club slipped out of existence after it failed to attend the league AGM in June.

The end of the road for Rossendale United as the main stand burns to the ground in January 2012.

Rossendale United's Greatest Players

(Qualification 300 appearances or 100 goals)

Roger Stott

The unfortunately nicknamed Raper Stott, the son of the club chairman made his debut on New Years day 1903 as a late stand in for the injured Jimmy Howard in a 1-1 draw with Nelson. A keen amateur with Newchurch Rovers he played a further six games towards the end of the 1903/04 season and impressed enough to be signed for the following season. He soon established himself at centre half where his calmness and organisation skills stood out. He was a virtual ever present for the next seven seasons remaining loyal to the club and playing as an amateur after all professional contracts were cancelled by the FA over non-payment of wages in 1910. He missed the 1912 Junior Cup triumph through injury but won the Rossendale charity cup on four occasions. He left to join local rivals Haslingden for the 1912/13 season before returning the following season to help Rossendale gain promotion back to division one of the Lancashire combination. He retired from football at the outbreak of World War One after becoming the first Rossy player to make 300 appearances for the club.

Playing Record:

Season	League	Cup	Total
1902/03	1-0		1-0
1903/04	6-0		6-0
1904/05	26-2	2-0	28-2
1905/06	34-0	4-0	38-0
1906/07	34-0	10-1	44-1
1907/08	36-0	5-0	41-0
1908/09	33-1	4-0	37-1
1909/10	28-0	4-0	32-0
1910/11	28-0	3-0	31-0
1911/12	27-0	6-0	33-0
1913/14	20-1		20-1
Total	273-4	38-1	311-5

William Ingham

Signed from Freetown prior to the 1905/06 season the skilful inside forward with an eye for goal became an instant hit with the Rossy supporters scoring a hat trick against St Helens Recs at Dark Lane

in only his second game. He went on to become the first Rossy player to score 20 league goals in a season and broke the clubs goalscoring record finishing with 27 in his first season. A virtual ever present over the next five seasons he twice topped the 20 goal a season mark and when he was forced to leave the club after the financial crisis of 1910 he had scored a 109 goals in 218 appearances for the club.

After initially signing for Accrington Stanley for the 1910/11 season he was enticed south to Norwich City then in the Southern League by former Rossy official Bert Stansfield who was then the Norwich manager, along with ex Rossy players Eddie Whiteside and Ralph Bibby. He enjoyed a successful spell at Norwich twice representing the Southern League representative side against the Irish League and Scottish league, before returning north to find work at the end of World War one. He re-signed for Rossy in September 1919 and played a key role as the team re-established themselves in the Lancashire Combination after a difficult start, scoring 16 goals. He finally retired at the end of the 1920/21 season after scoring a then club record 128 goals in 270 appearances with ten hat-ticks including twice scoring four goals in a game. He won the Rossendale Charity cup on three occasions.

Season	League	Cup	Total
1905/06	37-21	3-6	40-27
1906/07	38-21	10-5	48-26
1907/08	38-10	5-4	43-14
1908/09	38-12	6-4	44-16
1909/10	37-22	6-4	43-26
1919/20	30-16	1-0	31-16
1920/21	20-3	1-0	21-3
Total	238-105	32-23	270-128

Teddy Hill

A former Bury reserve player Hill had quit football to concentrate on his business interests playing occasional games for Ramsbottom traders association and cricket for Ramsbottom, until he was enticed back to the game as Rossy rebuilt a team after the financial crisis in 1910. Hill made his debut in the third game of the 1910/11 season scoring a hat trick in the 7-1 thrashing of Padiham and never looked back becoming an instant favourite with the fans. A fast and skilfull forward with a poacher's instinct in front of goal Hill scored 22 goals in his first season despite missing several games due to his business and cricket commitments. The following season he topped the 20 goal mark once again including eight in the successful Lancashire junior Cup run which saw Hill turn in a man of the match performance and score the winning goal in the final against Eccles. Hill missed the first half of the 1912/13 season through injury and despite scoring 18 goals in just 21 games he could not prevent Rossy being relegated back to division two of the Lancashire Combination. He enjoyed his best season in 1913/14 scoring 27 goals in 30 games and firing Rossy back into the top flight of the Combination. During the season Hill turned down several offers from league clubs to turn professional citing his business interests as the main reason to stay at Dark Lane. The 1914/15 season saw Hill score just 14 goals in the league as Rossy struggled to put out a regular line up, but he enjoyed great success in the Junior cup as his 10 goals in four games including two hat-tricks once again fired Rossy into the final. He was unable to find the net in the final as Rossy went down 3-2 to Skelmersdale. The following season with the Lancashire Combination regionalised due to the war Hill played just five games scoring 1 goal before answering his countries call to arms. Overall Hill scored 118 goals in just 158 games before the war cut short his career.

Season	League	Cup	Total
1910/11	24-18	4-4	28-22
1911/12	27-15	8-8	35-23
1912/13	21-18	3-0	24-18
1913/14	25-22	5-5	30-27
1914/15	29-14	7-11	36-25
1915/16	5-1		5-1
Total	131-88	27-28	158-116

Mick Toman

A native of Newry in Northern Ireland Mick originally came to England for a trial with Football League new boys Nelson in 1921, but failed to earn a contract so signed for Rossy, settling in Stacksteads where he was to spend the rest of his life. A hardworking and skilfull inside forward Toman soon established himself in the side. The 1922/23 season saw him first show his goal scoring prowess forming an effective partnership with fellow Irishman Paddy Quigley he finished the season with 16 goals. Now established at inside left the following season he formed a dynamic left sided partnership with winger Jimmy Kellett as Rossy built a team capable of challenging for the title. The 1925/26 season saw him score 22 goals and the following season he led Rossy to their only Lancashire Combination title scoring 32 league goals. The goals continued to flow as he led the club to cup success in the Lancashire Combination Cup and East Lancs Charity Cup. He broke Raper Stott's appearance record and became the first Rossy player to score 150 goals during the 1929/30 season. He gradually dropped deeper taking a playmaker role as the club struggled to assemble a team to regain the glories of the 1920's. As his career wound down, he took over as player manager in October 1933 and made only occasional appearances after that. He achieved some success as manager leading them to a fifth place in the 1934/35 season and leading them to great success in the Lancashire Senior Cup where league clubs Burnley, Bolton, Preston and Man Utd were all defeated as the club twice reached the quarter finals. He managed the club until December 1936 when the constant struggle with cost cutting measures and boardroom interference meant the sale of star forward Cyril Crawshaw to Rochdale and a subsequent row over the wage bill was the final straw and led to an acrimonious parting of the ways. Toman's fifteen year stay at the club saw him make a then club record 467 appearances scoring 172 goals for the club. Tragically despite serving on the LFA council and having an advisory role at Bacup for a time he was never fully reconciled with Rossendale United before he died in 1964.

Season	League	Cup	Total
1921/22	27-4	4-0	31-4
1922/23	32-16	7-0	39-16
1923/24	30-4	8-5	38-9
1924/25	32-15	7-3	39-18
1925/26	33-18	6-4	39-22
1926/27	36-32	6-2	42-34
1927/28	35-20	11-5	46-25
1928/29	32-13	4-0	36 13
1929/30	36-13	4-1	40-14
1930/31	36-2	5-0	41-2
1931/32	32-8	3-1	35-9
1932/33	26-5	4-0	30-5
1933/34	7-0	1-0	8-0
1935/36	2-1	1-0	3-1
Total	396-151	71-21	467-172

John Williams

Pendlebury born Williams was signed from Bacup in October 1923, a big powerful centre forward he took time to settle into the side, but once he had built an understanding with fellow new signings Peter Cowper and Albert Walmsley, he played a key role as Rossendale finished the season strongly to finish in fifth place and win the Roscoe Cup. He finished with 14 goals from 32 games and his excellent link up play in the forward line had attracted the attention of Burnley who signed him for a small fee during the close season. He broke into the Burnley first team towards the end of the 1924/25 season scoring 2 goals in his second game a 5-4 win over West Ham. He soon lost his place after four games and never made another first team appearance in his three year stay at Turf Moor. Upon his release from Burnley Williams signed for Darwen but was enticed back to reigning Champions Rossy in September 1927 making an instant impact with two goals in his first game and 6 in his first four games back at the club. Now even stronger and more powerful Williams was a veritable goalscoring machine smashing club goalscoring records on his way to 48 league goals in just 33 games and finishing with 53 from 43 games overall as Rossy reached three cup finals. Unfortunately, Williams was unable to find the net in either the junior Cup final or the Lancashire Combination Cup final as Rossy lost narrowly to Lancaster and Horwich respectively. However, his extra time goal against Darwen in the East Lancs Charity Cup did bring some silver ware back to Dark Lane. The following season he was even better smashing his own record in bagging 52 goals in 35 league games finishing the season with a club record 56 goals in 40 games including the winning goal against Southport Reserves in the Lancashire Combination Cup final. He started the 1929/30 season in similar vein with 9 goals in six games before work commitments saw him leave the club his departure spelling the end the Clubs successful era in the late 1920's. Overall Williams scored 132 goals in just 121 games for the club bagging eight hat tricks as well as scoring 4 on eight occasions. He returned to football helping Clitheroe to the 1931 Junior Cup Final before retiring through injury.

Season	League	Cup	Total
1923/24	27-12	5-2	32-14
1927/28	33-48	10-5	43-53
1928/29	35-52	5-4	40-56
1929/30	5-8	1-1	6-9
Total	100-120	21-12	121-132

Jack Isherwood

 Jack Isherwood made his debut on New Year's Day 1937 as a late replacement for Tom Slater scoring in a 7-3 defeat at Marine. He had to wait till April for his next appearance in the Lancashire Combination Cup semi-final at Bacup where he created the only goal for Horace Stannard to fire Rossy into the final for the first time since 1929. He retained his place for the final against Barrow Reserves scoring in a 3-1 defeat at South Liverpool. The following season he moved to Centre Forward and topped scored with 32 goals his pace and nerveless finishing leaving defenders floundering. The following season he moved to inside left and in partnership with Herbert Fox continued to hit the back of the net bagging 40 goals in all competitions.

The outbreak of war brought an end to normal football, but the Lancashire Combination continued to run a limited programme and Isherwood continued to find the net scoring 27 goals in 24 games. The following season the club entered the Manchester League and Isherwood who worked in a reserved occupation was available for most of it scoring 53 goals in just 30 games including a club record nine in the Gylgrist Cup semi-final when Rossy beat Droylesden 15-4. He also bagged one in the 5-4 win over Hyde Utd in the final. The 1941–42 season saw Rossy return to the reformed Combination and Isherwood bagged another 36 goals in 29 games including Rossy's only goal in a 5-1 defeat in the Combination Cup final against a very strong Blackpool Services team. The following season with football now becoming more restricted Isherwood bagged 19 goals in 20 games. The 1943/44 season saw Isherwood's appearances restricted after his conscription into the forces he scored 11 goals in 8 appearances as Rossy won a league and cup double in a much weakened Lancashire Combination. The following season the Combination was suspended and Rossy competed in the Burnley and District league and Isherwood managed 7 appearances and 1 goal whilst on leave. The following season Isherwood returned home in early 1946 to resume his goal scoring form bagging 8 goals in 16 games mainly in cup competitions as Rossy reached the Combination cup semi-finals and Junior cup final where the club lost to Chorley in a replay Isherwood featuring in both games. The following season with football returning to normal Isherwood scored 8 goals in 19 games before he was tempted to join local rivals Bacup Borough his goals helping them secure their only Lancashire Combination title. In all Isherwood scored 237 goals in just 262 appearances for Rossy, with 155 of these goals being scored in wartime football.

Season	League	Cup	Total
1936/37	2-1	2-1	4-2
1937/38	42-30	6-2	48-32
1938/39	42-38	5-2	47-40

1939/40	17-18	7-9	24-27
1940/41	27-40	3-13	30-53
1941/42	14-23	15-13	29-36
1942/43	9-9	11-10	20-19
1943/44	2-2	6-9	8-11
1944/45	6-1	1-0	7-1
1945/46	3-1	13-7	16-8
1946/47	18-7	1-1	19-8
Total	192-170	70-67	262-237

JOHNNY CLARK

 Johnny was born in Liverpool in 1926 and moved to the valley as a child. He was signed by Rossendale in 1946 from Bury where he had played for the reserves and went on to make a club record 777 appearances for the club between 1946 and 1965 most of them at left back. Johnny made his debut in a 2-2 draw at Morecambe on the 11th January 1947 and established himself as first choice left back the following season, a position he was to hold for the next fifteen seasons.

His first goal for the club came in a 3-2 win over Wigan Athletic in 1952 and he was to add twelve more over his career. He missed just two games in the 1954/55 season as Rossendale finished runners up in the Lancashire Combination his highest finish during his career. He also played a key role as Rossy won the Lancashire Combination Division Two Championship and promotion in 1956/57. During the second half of the 1962/63 season at the age of 37 he lost his place at left back to Graeme Lord but returned midway through the following season to help out the club at right back. The 1964/65 season was to be his last making a dozen appearances at full back, he made his final appearance on the last day of the season in a 3-2 defeat at Dark Lane against South Liverpool. Over the course of his extensive career his loyalty to the club saw him play anywhere across the back four as well as a stand in centre forward scoring in a 5-2 win at Wigan athletic in 1959. He also helped out by playing in goal on four occasions later in his career.

As well as record 641 league games, Johnny made a record 136 cup appearances including a record 38 FA Cup appearances. He picked runners up medals in the Lancashire Combination Cup against Bangor City in 1949 and the Lancashire Junior Cup against New Brighton in 1957. He also had winner's medals in the East Lancashire Charity Cup in 1957 and 1958.

Season	League	Cup	Total
1946/47	9-0	1-0	10-0
1947/48	24-0	7-0	31-0
1948/49	28-0	13-0	41-0
1949/50	35-4	7-0	42-4

1950/51	40-1	9-0	49-1
1951/52	39-1	6-0	45-1
1952/53	41-0	5-0	46-0
1953/54	37-1	7-0	44-1
1954/55	40-0	6-0	46-0
1955/56	38-0	7-0	45-0
1956/57	28-0	14-1	42-1
1957/58	36-4	11-0	47-4
1958/59	39-1	7-0	46-1
1959/60	41-0	9-0	50-0
1960/61	39-0	10-0	49-0
1961/62	38-0	3-0	41-0
1962/63	36-0	5-0	41-0
1963/64	33-0	4-0	37-0
1964/65	20-0	5-0	25-0
Total	641-12	136-1	777-13

Derek Hughes

Derek was signed in the summer of 1952 after his release by Bury FC where he had played reserve team football. A powerfully built left half Hughes made his debut as a makeshift centre forward against Accrington Stanley reserves on the 25th August 1952 scoring in a 2-1 defeat he kept his place at centre forward for three games also scoring in a 2-1 win over Barrow reserves. He then dropped out of the side before finally establishing himself in his favoured half back role in October. He completed 37 games in his first season and was an established regular at half back before moving to centre half during the 1954/55 season where he missed just one game as Rossy finished runners up in the Lancashire combination. He also won a Division two championship medal in 1957 and was a member of the side that finished runners up to New Brighton in the Lancashire Junior cup in 1957 and won the North East Lancs cup that same season. He lost his place at centre half during the 1959/60 season to new signing Kingsley Davies and finished the season in the forward line as he bagged five goals. The following season saw him play just eight games as he filled in defence or midfield playing his last game against Burscough in February 1961 before leaving the club. Overall, Derek played a total 329 games scoring 10 goals in a nine year stay at Dark Lane.

1952/53	32-3	5-0	37-3
1953/54	40-1	7-0	47-1
1954/55	41-0	7-0	48-0
1955/56	32-1	6-0	38-1
1956/57	32-0	13-0	45-0
1957/58	31-0	8-0	39-0
1958/59	32-0	7-0	39-0

1959/60	23-5	4-0	27-5
1960/61	8-0	1-0	9-0
Total	271-10	58-0	329-10

Tommy Willighan

Tommy a Burnley Junior was signed in the summer of 1955 after his release by the clarets a tough inside forward with a ferocious shot he scored a brace on his debut in a 3-3 draw with Marine on the opening day of the 1955/56 season. Overall, he scored 18 goals in 42 games in what was a disappointing season that saw Rossy relegated to the Lancashire Combination second division. The following season he scored 11 goals in 37 games as Rossy won the second division championship although injuries and suspension saw Tommy miss several games during the second half of the season, although he did return to the side for the Junior Cup final defeat to New Brighton.

The following season saw Tommy bag 14 goals as Rossy re- established themselves in the top flight. The 1958/59 season saw Tommy take a deeper role as a midfield enforcer a move that cemented his reputation as one of the Combinations hard men. The signing of Billy Blackburn saw Tommy move to centre forward in October 1959 as he formed a prolific goal scoring partnership with Bob Scott. A move back to inside forward did not diminish Tommy's scoring prowess as he topped 20 goals in a season for the only time in his career during the 1961/62 season. The following season Tommy became the seventh Rossy player to score 100 goals for the club when he netted with a typical thunderous volley against Burscough. Tommy moved to Horwich RMI during the summer of 1963 after scoring a 115 goals in 323 games for the club.

Season	League	Cup	Total
1955/56	36-11	6-7	42-18
1956/57	25-8	12-3	37-11
1957/58	39-13	8-1	47-14
1958/59	35-3	5-0	40-3
1959/60	33-15	9-2	42-17
1960/61	30-10	6-3	36-13
1961/62	37-19	3-3	40-22
1962/63	36-15	3-0	38-15
Total	271-94	52-19	323-113

Dennis Ormerod

Local lad Dennis Ormerod was called up to replace the injured Bill Whitehead against Ashton Utd on the 28th December 1957, and did enough at left half to retain his place for the next game against Southport reserves. A strong resolute half back Dennis made a further five league appearances and picked up a winners medal in the North East Lancashire Cup as Rossy thrashed Accrington Stanley reserves 6-1 in the final.

The following season Dennis broke into the side at the beginning of October after Bill Whitehead left the club and established himself at right half helping the club move up the table after a poor start. Dennis scored his first goal for the club in the 11-2 drubbing of Fleetwood. Dennis was now a fixture in the side and was to miss just 13 games over the next eight seasons. Unfortunately for Dennis his spell at the club was not a golden era as the financial difficulties began to bite. However, despite the difficulties the club usually finished mid table and avoided relegation problems, with Dennis's sterling efforts in the half back line playing a significant part in this. Dennis played his last game for the club in a 4-3 defeat at Kirkby Town on the 1st December 1967. In all he played a total of 447 league and cup games for the club which at the time put him third behind legends Johnny Clark and Mick Toman in the all time appearance list.

Season	League	Cup	Total
1957/58	7-0	2-0	9-0
1958/59	36-1	5-0	41-1
1959/60	40-4	10-0	50-4
1960/61	35-2	8-0	43-2
1961/62	42-3	3-0	45-3
1962/63	41-0	5-0	46-0
1963/64	41-4	4-1	45-5
1964/65	41-2	8-1	49-3
1965/66	41-0	7-0	48-0
1966/67	42-2	8-0	50-2
1967/68	16-0	5-0	21-0
Total	382-18	65-2	447-20

Bob Scott

Brother to Rangers, Everton and Scotland forward Alex, Bob Scott left his Falkirk home to try and earn a professional contract with Bury in 1956. After being released at the end of his trial period Bob found work in the factories of Rossendale and continued his football with Bacup Borough where his goals attracted the attention of Lancaster City where he finished the 1958/59 season. Unable to settle at Lancaster Bob was one of the key signings for the 1959/60 season.

Of average height but strongly built Bob's speed of mind as well as speed of foot turned him into a real penalty area predator as he smashed the Clubs goalscoring record with 72 goals in just 51 games during the 59/60 season helping the club to a fifth place finish and a Junior cup semi final. He followed it up with another 44 goals the next season, but a leaky defence saw the club finish sixteenth. Despite the attentions of several other clubs Bob remained with Rossy and scored another 45 goals as the club had a better season finishing sixth in the 61/62 season. The 1962/63 saw Scott bag another 48 goals as he broke the club goalscoring record passing the 200 mark in just four seasons. With the club in severe financial difficulties, they were unable to keep hold of their star asset and he signed for Nelson who saw the forward as the key to their title ambitions. Fortunately for Rossy things did not go as planned and

Bob did not settle at Nelson and returned to Dark Lane during Christmas 1963 with Rossy in eighteenth position and in a relegation dog fight. He returned to the side against his former club Nelson on the 28th December and bagged a hat-trick in a vital 3-2 win. He went on to net 14 goals in twenty two games as the club comfortably avoided relegation.

With the financial position still perilous the club were unable to keep Bob who moved to Horwich RMI for the 64/65 season. In just four and half seasons Bob had scored an immense 223 goals for the club in just 203 games, 182 in league games. In that time, he had scored 16 hat-tricks, 4 goals on two occasions and 5 goals three times.

Season	League	Cup	Total
1959/60	40-51	11-21	51-72
1960/61	36-33	12-11	48-44
1961/62	40-43	2-2	42-45
1962/63	40-42	5-6	45-48
1963/64	20-13	2-1	22-14
Total	176-182	32-41	208-223

John Pearson

Wiganer Pearson was a Busby babe at Manchester United, originally a right winger he lost his place in the Man Utd pecking order to a certain George Best and upon his release signed for Third Division York City, in the summer of 1965. He became York's first ever substitute when he came on for his debut against Grimsby and went on to make 18 league and cup appearances scoring 4 goals during the season, which ended in relegation to division four. Unfortunately, he was not retained and he came home to Wigan. Now a pacey goalscoring inside forward he first came to Rossy's attention when he scored against them for Wigan Rovers on Boxing Day 1967. The following season manager Les Rigby made several attempts to sign John before finally getting his man in March 1969. He repaid the managers faith with a goal on his debut against Dukinfield Town and finished the season with 14 goals in just 14 appearances. The following season he bagged a total of 49 goals in all competitions, including six in a 10-0 romp against his old team Wigan Rovers.

The 1970/71 season saw Rossy embark on their first Cheshire league campaign and John formed part of a remarkable goalscoring triumvirate with Glyn Barker and Peter Bourne who scored a 102 goals between them as Rossy enjoyed their best season ever winning the Cheshire league and Lancashire Floodlight League Cup, in all John scored 40 goals in 59 appearances. The following season John continued his goalscoring exploits in tandem with Glyn Barker after Peter Bourne emigrated to Australia, bagging 38 goals in 52 games including eight in the epic FA Cup run which culminated in a second round defeat to Bolton Wanderers. By now John was a marked man and the rough treatment he received often meant he played on with knocks and the following season he was less effective and after scoring 11 goals in 15 games he was tempted to team up with former manager Les Rigby signing for Wigan for a reported fee of £500 in October. Things did not work out for John at Wigan and the club were delighted when he rejoined for the 1973/74 season, he had bagged 14 goals in 29 games as Rossy topped the table when he suffered a bad injury against New Brighton on Boxing day which effectively ended his season. With the financial situation becoming increasingly difficult Rossy were unable to keep Pearson who signed for Chorley, before finishing his career at Horwich RMI where alongside a host of former Rossy players he scored 29 goals as they won the Cheshire League in 1979. Overall, John scored 166 goals for Rossy in 215 appearances and throughout the 1970's was one of hottest goalscoring properties in North West non league football.

Season	League	Cup	Total
1968/69	14-14		14-14
1969/70	33-41	13-8	46-49
1970/71	38-23	20(1)-17	58(1)-40
1971/72	34(1)-21	17-17	51(1)-38
1972/73	10(1)-6	4-5	14(1)-11
1973/74	20-11	9-3	29-14
Total	149(2)-116	63(1)-50	212(3)-166

Bob Woods

Signed by Les Rigby prior to the 1969/70 season from Chorley, centre half Woods was to become one of Rossy's most loyal servants. He made his debut at Lytham on the 13th August 1969 scoring the only goal of the game and established himself as the lynch pin of the team for the next seven seasons, he was an ever present as Rossy won the Cheshire league title in 1971 making a mammoth 65 appearances that season also winning the Lancashire Floodlight league and the Cheshire league Challenge shield. The following season Woods struggled with injuries at the start of the season but still played a key role as the club progressed to the second round of the FA Cup and his return to full fitness saw the club embark on a ten match winning run that saw the club finish runners up behind Rhyl in the Cheshire league, he also picked up another winners medal as the club defeated Wigan athletic to pick up the Lancs FA floodlight KO cup. The following season Bob once again topped 50 appearances and he picked up more silver ware as he captained the team to glory in the Lancashire junior Cup. 1973/74 saw Bob once again make 53 appearances as the club finished runners up to Marine in the league, unfortunately injuries meant Bob missed the heroic 5-0 second leg win over Burscough that saw Rossy pick up the Cheshire League Cup and the Lancs floodlight cup win a week later. The 1974/75 season saw Rossy struggle as the financial pressure began to bite, but Bob stayed loyal and had a spell as caretaker manager after the departure of Alan Kirkman until the appointment of Don Wilson. The 1975/76 season was the last hurrah of the great side of the early 70's and Woods once again played a key role as he led the team to the FA Cup first round his performance in both games against Blyth Spartans being arguably the best ever by a centre half in a Rossy shirt. As the financial plight became clear the side was broken up and when manager Wilson left in March Woods once again stepped up as caretaker manager. He retained the job for the following season and despite a lack of funds made a promising start but a run of four defeats and an early FA Cup exit saw him asked to rejoin the ranks as he was replaced by Eric Roberts. With age and injuries beginning to take their toll Bob started the 1977/78 season helping on the coaching side and as an occasional squad player however the mass walkout of players in February 1978 saw him once more step into the breach as player-manager, he scraped a scratch squad together to complete the fixture against Marine that ended in a 14-2 defeat but gradually he rebuilt the team and stabilised the club. Woods tried to continue the rebuilding job the following season but with little money to spend it was an uphill struggle and despite wins over fellow strugglers that kept the club out of the relegation places a run of five heavy defeats against the better teams at the end of 1978 saw Woods tender his resignation and leave the club, he returned a few weeks later for testimonial event organised by the club in recognition of his service to Rossendale United, but sadly was never seen at Dark Lane again. Overall, in ten seasons at the club Bob played a total 411 games scoring 17 goals and won a host of medals.

Season	League	Cup	Total
1969/70	35-4	15-1	50-5
1970/71	42-2	23-1	65-3
1971/72	28-0	17-0	45-0
1972/73	38-0	12-0	50-0
1973/74	38-1	15-0	53-1
1974/75	34-1	10-0	44-1
1975/76	34-2	10-1	44-3
1976/77	25(1)-2	4-1	29(1)-3
1977/78	17(2)-1	6-0	23(2)-1
1978/79	5-0		5-0
Total	296(3)-13	112-4	408(3)-17

Glyn Barker

 A former Blackburn Rovers apprentice Glyn had spells at Chorley and Great Harwood before signing for Rossy in the summer of 1970. Not particularly tall for a centre forward Barker had a prodigious leap that often saw him out jump taller defenders and an uncanny knack for finding space in the penalty area. He formed and unstoppable forward line with John Pearson and Peter Bourne scoring 14 league goals as they fired Rossy to the Cheshire league title he added another 18 cup goals to his tally as he finished the season with 32 goals in 63 appearances.

An unselfish player he formed successful goalscoring partnerships with whomever he partnered upfront and scored 20 plus goals a season in each of his five full seasons at the club and played in every cup final for the club between 1970 and 75 scoring vital goals in most of them. He was also a key member of both FA cup run teams although an injury against Blyth in the replay meant he was not at his best when the team played Shrewsbury in the FA cup first round in 1975. He played his last game for the club against Burscough in December 1975 leaving to join Ashton Utd as the club drastically cut spending after the FA Cup run.

He later teamed up with former manager Alan Kirkman and several ex Rossy players to help Horwich RMI win the Cheshire League title before retiring from the game. His son Ian also played for Rossy and Glyn was often seen on Dark Lane cheering his son on.

Season	League	Cup	Total
1970/71	39(1)-14	23-18	62(1)-32
1971/72	38-21	20-9	58-30

1972/73	41-24	14-8	55-32
1973/74	37-20	19-9	56-29
1974/75	36-19	10-3	46-22
1975/76	10-4	10-5	20-9
Total	201(1)-102	96-52	297(1)-154

Billy Greenan

 A Scot Billy Greenan was signed from neighbours Bacup during the summer of 1970 to boost the squad prior to the clubs initial Cheshire league campaign. Originally a right winger he took time to displace Jimmy Hammill and Gordon Fisher but established himself in the Championship side during the run in, making 31 appearances including 7 from the bench he also made 19 cup appearances picking up a winners medal in the Lancashire FA league cup. His combative nature and incisive passing saw him establish himself in the side in a midfield role as he became a key member of the great side of the early 70's, playing a major role in the FA Cup runs of 1971 and 75 and picking up winners medals in the Junior cup, Cheshire league cup Lancashire Floodlit cup twice as well as two Cheshire league runners up medals.

His best season was 1973–74 when he scored 27 goals in all competitions from central midfield. He left the club briefly to join Ashton Utd after the 75 cup run as the clubs cost cutting measures took effect. But returned the following season, he then left to join Horwich RMI in December 1977 teaming up with ex Rossy manager Alan Kirkman and several old teammates to win the Cheshire league again in 1979. He spent four seasons at Horwich before finishing his career at Stalybridge Celtic and Whitworth Valley where he was manager. He returned to Dark Lane in the summer of 1986 as Steve Connaghan's assistant manager and enjoyed more success as the club won the North west counties league. Well known and respected in local football circles he was to die suddenly in 2010.

Season	League	Cup	Total
1970/71	24(7)-5	16(3)-7	40(10)-12
1971/72	31(1)-3	18(1)-4	49(2)-7
1972/73	30(1)-3	12-1	42(1)-4
1973/74	37-22	15-5	52-27
1974/75	34-6	12-2	46-8
1975/76	12-2	12-0	24-2
1976/77	34-5	5-2	39-7
1977/78	15-1	4-1	19-2
Total	227(9)-47	94(4)-22	321(13)-69

Mick Gardiner

Manager Bob Woods signed young forward Micky upon his release from Preston NE as he attempted to rebuild the team during the disastrous 77/78 campaign. He made his debut alongside Francis Lee in a 6-1 defeat to Formby and scored his first goals for the club in wins over Hyde and Winsford as the club salvaged some pride with a strong finish to the season. He remained a regular over the next three seasons under several managers mainly as a midfielder or wide attacking player before being converted to right back by Glyn Watson during the 80/81 season. He was a key member of the successful 81/82 team that finished fifth in the Cheshire League and reached the second round of the FA Trophy. He helped the club win promotion from the NWCFL second division in 85/86 and was made club captain and moved to a sweeper role by new manager Steve Connaghan the following season.

His calm leadership, vision and skill on the ball made him ideal for the role of sweeper and he led the club to runners up spot a in 1987/88 and ultimately to the NWCFL championship the following season. Injuries began to limit his appearances as the club established themselves in the Northern Premier League and he left the club at the end of the season to become Steve Connaghan's assistant at Salford, but not before enjoying a well earned testimonial game against Joe Royle's Oldham. His unstinting loyalty to the club saw him finish with 464 appearances for the club behind fellow legends Johnny Clark and Mick Toman.

Season	League	Cup	Total
1977/78	9-2	-	9-2
1978/79	36(1)-6	7-4	43(1)-10
1979/80	22(1)-2	7-0	29(1)-2
1980/81	28-0	7-0	35-0
1981/82	35-0	7-0	42-0
1982/83	26-0	8(1)-1	34(1)-1
1983/84	28-1	3-0	31-1
1984/85	27-0	5-0	32-0
1985/86	31(1)-1	13-0	44(1)-1
1986/87	33-1	17-0	50-1
1987/88	33-0	19-0	52-0
1988/89	23(1)-1	8(2)-0	31(3)-1
1989/90	18(2)-0	3(2)-0	21(4)-0
Total	349(16)-14	104(5)-5	453(11)-19

Paul Beck

One of new manager Dave O Neill's first acts upon becoming manager in January 1985 was to sign forward Paul Beck from neighbours Accrington Stanley to bolster a shot shy attack and it paid instant dividends as his 10 goals in 16 games ensured survival in the NWCFL division two. The following season in partnership with the mercurial Jimmy Clarke he scored 32 goals in all competitions as the club won promotion to the NWC top division and reached the league cup semi finals. The following season he followed manager O Neill to Clitheroe but returned to Dark Lane for the 1987/88 season by this time

Rossy had three top quality strikers with Jocky Wylie joining Beck and Clarke in the competition for places in the team and manager Steve Connaghan had his hands full keeping them all happy, nonetheless Beck scored 21 goals in all competitions as Rossy missed out on promotion to the Northern premier League on goal difference to big spending local rivals Colne Dynamoes.

The 1988/89 season saw Rossy comfortably clinch the NWCL Championship with Beck forming a devastating partnership with Wylie. Beck finished the season with 26 goals in all competitions. The following season saw Beck reach the 40 goals mark, the first since Johnny Pearson nineteen seasons earlier, as the club established themselves in the Northern Premier first division. Unfortunately, the club were unable to hold on to their prize asset as he returned to his hometown club of Accrington Stanley for £1000 fee in the summer of 1990. He enjoyed a successful six years at Stanley where he scored over a 100 goals before retiring from senior non league football. He did make one further appearance for Rossy on loan during the 93/94 season. Paul Beck was one of the hottest properties in northwest non league football in the 1980's and early 1990's with an insatiable appetite for goals, which saw him score over 100 goals for both his two main clubs where he was adored and acquired legend status.

Season	League	Cup	Total
1984/85	16-10	-	16-10
1985/86	32(1)-25	9(1)-7	41(2)-32
1987/88	25(1)-12	12(2)-9	37(3)-21
1988/89	32(1)-20	9(1)-6	41(2)-26
1989/90	41-26	14-14	55-40
1993/94	1-0		1-0
Total	147(3)-93	44(4)-36	191(7)-129

Craig Sargeson

Craig joined Rossy in January 1998 as a teenager initially to join the new youth set up and reserve team but within a month of the start of the 1998/99 season he had broken into the first team and established himself in the forward line scoring 22 goals in his first season. The following season the major investment in the club by Andrew Connolly saw an influx of new players, but Sargey kept his place and thrived alongside the experienced Jim McLuskie scoring 39 goals in all competitions as the club finished fifth in the league and reached the NWC Floodlit Cup Final. The following season he finished the League's leading goalscorer with 39 goals as the club clinched the North West Counties title and promotion. This saw him become the youngest player to score 100 goals for Rossy.

The move up in standard saw him find goals harder to come by especially as he had to lead the line himself, but he still scored 22 goals. His final season at Rossy was a difficult one as managerial changes and positional ones saw him play deeper or out wide however, he still finished with 15 goals.

He decided to try his luck elsewhere moving to Witton and then spent several seasons at Clitheroe moving to deeper role before finishing his career at Bamber Bridge. Sargey had ice in his veins when it came to goalscoring for Rossy and his talents attracted several football league clubs including Wigan where he had a trial, but a perceived lack of pace meant there was no offer of a contract. He also had a very shrewd football brain which came to the fore when he moved to a deeper position later in his career.

Season	League	Cup	Total
1998/99	33(1) – 21	9 - 1	42(1)- 22
1999/00	40-26	15(1)-13	55(1)-39
2000/01	38(3)-34	7(1)-5	45(4)-39
2001/02	35(6)-15	13(1)-7	48(7)-22
2002/03	35(7)-13	11-2	46(7)-15
Total	181(17)-109	55(3)-28	236(20()-137

Miscellany

Players who have scored 50 or more goals for Rossendale United

name	years	gls	apps	pos
Jack Isherwood	1936–47	237	262	f
Bob Scott	1959–64	223	208	f
Mick Toman	1921–36	172	467	if
Johnny Pearson	1968–74	166	215	f
Glyn Barker	1970–76	154	298	f
Craig Sargeson	1998–2003	137	256	f
John Williams	1923–30	132	121	f
Paul Beck	1985–93	129	198	f
Willie Ingham	1905–21	128	270	f
Teddy Hill	1910–16	116	158	f
Tommy Willighan	1955–63	113	323	if
Frank Campbell	1956–60	94	160	cf
Jack Kellett	1921–29	93	267	f
Jimmy Clarke	1985–93	93	116	f
Geoff Cookson	1956–59	92	115	f
John Wylie	1984–90	82	149	f
Dick Haworth	1936–46	78	152	f
Billy Greenan	1970–78	69	334	mf
Frank Ramsbottom	1939–44	69	114	f
Tommy Appleton	1960–63	62	136	If
Lol Cook	1908–10	62	63	cf
Norman Berry	1947–54	61	236	if
Alf Davies	1948–50	61	62	f
Bobby Grimshaw	1972–90	58	247	mf
Phil Eastwood	2006–10	57	141	f
Peter Bourne	1968–71	55	157	f
Eddie Hartley	1954–64	54	130	f
Chris Brooks	2001–11	52	189	mf

Players who have made a 100 or more appearances for Rossendale United

name	years	apps	pos
Johnny Clark	1946–65	777	fb
Mick Toman	1921–36	467	if
Micky Gardiner	1977–90	464	d
Dennis Ormerod	1957–68	447	hb
Bob Woods	1969–79	411	d
Billy Greenan	1970–78	334	mf
Derek Hughes	1952–61	329	hb
Tommy Willighan	1955–63	323	if
Raper Stott	1902–14	311	d
Glyn Barker	1970–76	298	f
Steve Molloy	1946–64	288	hb
Kenny Fletcher	1970–76	273	mf-d
Willie Ingham	1905–21	270	f
Hilbert(harry) Barnes	1934–42	267	hb
Jack Kellett	1921–29	267	f
Jack Isherwood	1936–47	262	f
Craig Sargeson	1998–2003	256	f
Jimmy Wishart	1919–27	250	ch
Bobby Grimshaw	1972–90	247	mf
Walter Taylor	1912–25	245	fb
Steve Walker	1984–97	243	mf
Dennis Crompton	1970–75	240	d
John Wood	1970–75	239	glk
Norman Berry	1947–54	236	if
Steve Hobson	1984–93	218	glk
Johnny Pearson	1968–74	215	f
Wayne Howarth	1984–94	214	mf
Mark Andrews	1996–2006	209	glk
Bob Scott	1959–64	208	f
Harry Hall	1919–30	207	if
Tommy Ross	1971–76	201	mf
Paul Beck	1985–93	198	f
Frank O Kane	1978–84	198	f
Antony Flanagan	1986–92	197	d
Jason Heffernan	1998–2003	196	d
Chris Brooks	2001–11	189	mf
Matt Houldsworth	1999–2004	189	d

name	years	apps	pos
Jack Kirkbright	1925–30	188	d
Alex Binnie	1987–97	184	f
Barry Harrison	1964–68	178	d
Neil Yates	1985–93	174	d
Ken Bland	1957–61	173	glk
Jack Hitchen	1973–79	171	d
David Wild	1970–73	171	d
Jimmy Buchanan	1955–59	167	fb
Ged Walsh	1989–2003	165	mf
Tommy Aspin	1934–39	164	hb
Harry Evans	1954–58	163	hb
Percy Bury	1926–30	161	glk
Frank Campbell	1956–60	160	cf
Alf Berry	1906–10	159	if
Teddy Hill	1910–16	158	f
Peter Bourne	1968–71	157	f
Bill Craig	1947–51	156	fb
John Chapman	1920–26	153	hb
Harry Atherton	1948–52	152	glk
Alan Byrom	1980–90	152	d
David Crompton	1968–72	152	f
Dick Haworth	1936–46	152	f
Danny Heys	1997–2003	151	f
John Wylie	1984–90	149	f
Mark Kayley	1986–92	146	d
Matt Raywood	1997–06	144	d
Gordon Stones	1963–68	143	d
Dave O Neill	1972–86	142	mf
Phil Eastwood	2006–10	141	f
Frank Walkden	1926–30	139	hb
Peter cooper	1978–84	138	mf
Billy Cook	1904–1920	137	fb
Tommy Appleton	1960–63	136	lf
Edward Power	1939–46	135	glk
Harold Bell	1924–30	134	hb
Ralph Grimshaw	1933–36	134	hb
Andy Grimshaw	1985–2002	133	mf
Graham Walton	1978–84	133	f
Jimmy Wyatt	1911–15	133	glk
John Rushton	1923–26	131	fb
Eddie Hartley	1954–64	130	f

name	years	apps	pos
Jack Schofield	1937–42	130	hb
Bill O Laughlin	1957–60	129	f
Tom Whittaker	1933–36	128	d
Matt Knowles	1997–2003	127	mf
Billy Barker	1902–10	125	hb
Jerome Fitzgerald	1998–2002	124	d-mf
Joe Lyons	1925–32	124	d
Duncan McFadyen	1990–94	122	d
Benny Jones	1938–43	121	hb
Tommy Nuttall	1947–51	121	hb
John Williams	1923–30	121	f
Steve Cunningham	1999–2003	120	mf
Geoff Foster	1967–83	118	glk
Kingsley Davies	1959–63	117	d
Jimmy Clarke	1985–93	116	f
Geoff Cookson	1956–59	115	f
Paul Houldsworth	1996–2000	115	mf
Fred McGregor	1905–09	115	glk
Frank Crawshaw	1935–39	114	glk
Andy Derbyshire	1986–92	114	mf
Andy Hornsby	1985–90	114	d
Frank Ramsbottom	1939–44	114	f
Billy Blackburn	1957–61	113	d
Alex Jones	1907–10	111	if
Billy Palmer	1938–49	111	f
George Haigh	1947–50	109	hb
Jimmy Howard	1898–1903	109	if
Graeme Lord	1960–65	109	d
James Heywood	2007–10	109	d
Peter Vipham	1965–68	109	glk
John Ryder	1974–77	105	mf
Charlie Cowsill	1954–61	104	f
Tom Clarkson	2007–10	103	d
Darren Maloney	1996–99	103	f
Steve Parry	1989–92	103	f
Bernard Baldwin	1972–74	102	mf
Robert Arrowsmith	1903–06	100	glk
Steve Pickup	1995–99	100	d

Rossendale United managers

Up until the 1960's, apart from a few short term experiments with a team manager the team was usually selected by the committee with a trainer in charge of fitness and match day tactics. In the time prior to World War Two the two long serving trainers were Johnny Weir and Charlie Morris. The longest serving manager was Mick Toman who managed three years in charge. In the post war era. Roland Sharpe was secretary and committee member in charge of the team until the 1960's when the club introduced a coach or manager. In the modern era Steve Connaghan was the longest serving manager who managed nearly seven years in charge over two spells.

Managers

1905–07 John Watson	1986–90 Steve Connaghan
1911–12/13–15 William Cockerill	1990 Kevin Keelan
1932–33 Joe Campbell	1990–92 Steve Connaghan
1933 Eli Nuttall	1992 Ian Rishton(caretaker)
1933–36 Mick Toman	1992 Gary Peirce
1937 Reuben Butler	1993 Geoff Lutley
1937–38 L Cardwell	1993–94 Brent Peters
1961–63 Charlie Ferguson p/c	1994 Chris Nicholson
1963–67 Paddy Sowden p/m	1995 Gerry Keenan p/m
1967–68 Gordon Stone	1995 Scott Moore p/m
1968–72 Les Rigby	1995 Gary Blackshaw
1972–74 Alan Kirkman	1996–2000 Mickey Graham
1974 Bob Woods(caretaker)p/m	2000–02 Jim McLuskie
1975–76 Don Wilson	2002–03 Jim McBride
1976 Bob Woods p/m	2003 Paul Lynch
1976 Eric Roberts	2004 Jim McLuskie
1976–77 John Tomlinson	2004 Ashley Hoskin
1978 Bob Woods p/m	2004–05 Mark Molyneux p/m
1979–80 Tony Webber p/m	2005–08 Derek Egan
1980–82 Glyn Watson	2008–09 Phil Eastwood p/m
1982–84 Frank O Kane	2009–10 John Hughes
1984 Glyn Watson	2010 Paul Colgan/Gary Brown
1984–86 Dave O Neill p/m	2011 Chris Brooks/Jamie Baguley p/m

<u>Rossendale United Honours</u>

North West Counties League Division One Champions
1988/89 2000/01

North West Counties Division One Runners Up
1987/88 1993/94

North West Counties league Division Two Runners Up
1985/86

North West Counties Challenge Cup winners
1993/94

North West Counties Challenge Shield Winners
1988/89

North west Counties Floodlit trophy Runners Up
1999/2000

Cheshire League Champions
1970/71

Cheshire League Runners Up
1971/72 1973/74

Cheshire League Challenge Cup Winners
1973/74

Cheshire League Challenge Shield Winners
1970/71

Lancashire Combination Division One Champions
1926/27 1943/44

Lancashire Combination Division One Runners Up
1954/55

Lancashire Combination Division Two Champions
1956/57

Lancashire Combination Cup winners
1928/29 1943/44

Central Lancashire league Champions
1889/1900

Lancashire Junior Cup Winners
1911/12 1972/73

Lancashire Floodlit League Winners
1970/71

Lancashire Floodlit Cup Winners
1971/72 1973/74

North east Lancashire Cup Winners
1956/57 1957/58

Gyilgryt Cup Winners
1940/41

Ashworth Cup Winners
1972/73 1973/74

Rossendale Charity cup Winners
1900/01 1907/08 1908/09 1910/11

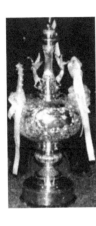

Premier
Challenge
Trophy

NWCFL
Division
Trophy

Rossendale Utd Test Cricketers

A football club the size of Rossendale United are probably unique in having five test cricketers turn out for them over the years.

The first was Bill Hitch born in Radcliffe, Bill moved south and made his name with Surrey for whom he played between 1907 and 1925 a fast bowler and powerful hitter Bill scored over 7000 runs and took 1387 wickets during his career. He was selected for the tour to Australia in 1911 and made his debut in the 2nd test at Melbourne helping England to an 8 wicket victory, he went on to play 3 Tests on the tour and a further 2 the following summer in the triangular tournament with Australia and South Africa. It was during the 1912/13 season that Bill turned out for Rossy, whilst visiting family in Rawtenstall, his brother Reg a keen cricketer himself for Rawtenstall was an official at Dark Lane and persuaded Bill to help out a struggling Rossendale who had yet to win a league game. He made his debut at centre forward on New Year's Day against St Helens and scored a goal in a narrow 2-1 defeat, his appearance adding several 100 to the gate he played two further games against Fleetwood and Eccles Borough which both ended in defeat before heading home. Bill played a further 2 tests for England after World War One and after retirement played some Lancashire League cricket.

A 19 year old Charlie Hallows had already made his debut for Lancashire CCC when he turned out on the left wing for Rossy in November 1914 in a 4-3 win over Haslingden in the Lancashire Junior cup. He went on to make a further 10 appearances that season. The following season he played a further 8 games scoring his only goal in a 2-1 defeat at Chorley. The Great War then put a stop to his sporting career and upon sports resumption Charlie concentrated on his cricket establishing himself as one of Lancashire's greatest batsmen. He made his test debut against the Australians in 1921 at Old Trafford but failed to keep his place. He made one more test appearance against the West Indies in 1928. Upon his retirement from cricket in 1932 Charlie soon established himself as one of the country's top coaches at Worcestershire and Lancashire.

The next Test player to don the blue and white stripes was South African Lennox S Brown. He played 7 games for Rossy at Centre Forward during the 1935/36 season scoring 4 goals including 2 in a 3-1 win over Preston North End in the Lancashire senior cup. Lennox had played two tests for South Africa in their tour of Australia and New Zealand in 1931–32 picking up 3 wickets. He soon moved to England where he combined professional football at Millwall, Huddersfield and Oldham with league cricket as a professional and was in a spell as Church professional in the Lancashire League when he signed for Rossy.

The same season Winston Place who turned out for Rossy in an East Lancashire Charity cup tie against Accrington Stanley Reserves and during the Second World war played a few more games for the club. However, it was as an opening partner of Cyril Washbrook with Lancashire that Winston was better known and his excellent batting earned him a place on the 1948 tour to the West Indies where he played 3 tests scoring a century in the last test. Unfortunately, the form of Len Hutton ensured this was to be his last test innings.

The final Rossy player to play test cricket is the legend that is David Lloyd, who played nine games for Rossy on the left hand side of the attack. He made his debut on the 7th of March 1963 in a 4-2 defeat at Dark Lane against Southport Reserves and scored his first goal for the club in a 4-1 win over Crompton Recs, he added two more goals including the winner in a shock 2-1 win over high flying Netherfield that secured Rossy's division one status. He played his last game for the club against Burscough on the14th of April before joining up with Lancashire for the forthcoming cricket season. He then concentrated on his cricket captaining Lancashire and playing nine tests scoring a double hundred against India before Lillee and Thomson literally knocked his test career on the head. David went on to manage both Lancashire and England before becoming one of the best pundits on TV. His son Ben also played for Rossendale in 2007.

Statistics and Records

Record League Victory

17 – 0 V Ashton Town Lancashire Combination 29/04/1911

Scorers Day 6, Ritchie 5, Hirst 3, Ward 2, Hopkinson

Team: Hannam, Beresford, Beasley, Ritchie, Hunt, Ward, Hopkinson, Day, Hirst, Hodgkinson.

Record Cup Victory

15 – 4 V Droyleden Gylgryst Cup semi final 5/04/1941

Scorers Isherwood 9, Ramsbottom3, Howarth 2, Hoyle

Team: Power, Jones, Winstanley, Schofield, Roberts, Macauley, Hoyle, Wolstenholme, Isherwood, Ramsbottom, Howarth

11 – 0 V Great Harwood Lancashire Junior Cup 14/01/1902

Scorers Morris 5, Bradley 3, Hoare, Waddington, Lucas

Team: Tattersall, Haslam, Higham, Heys, Howard, Lucas, Ashworth, Morris, Hoare, Bradley, Waddington

Record League defeat

14 – 0 V Morecambe Lancashire Combination 2/09/1967

Record goal scorers

6 or more goals in a game

9 Jack Isherwood V Droylesden (see above)

7 Dickie Day v Ashton Town 22/04/1911

6 Lol Cook v Bacup Borough 28/04/1909 Rossendale Charity Cup

6 Dickie Day v Ashton Town (see above)

6 Frank Ramsbottom v ROFSA United 2/01/1943 Lancashire Combination Cup

6 Clifford Greaves v Fleetwood 25/10/1958

6 Johnny Pearson v Wigan Rovers 30/01/1970

Goal scorers in a season

40 or more goals in a season

72 Bob Scott 1959/60 (51 games) goals per game 1.41

56 John Williams 1928/29 (42 games) goals per game 1.33

53 John Williams 1927/28 (43 games) goals per game 1.23

53 Jack Isherwood 1940/41 (30 games) goals per game 1.76

49 Johnny Pearson 1969/71 (46 games) goals per game 1.07

48 Bob Scott 1962/63 (45 games) goals per game 1.07

45 Lol Cook 1909/10 (42 games) goals per game 1.07

45 Alf Davies 1948/49 (42 games) goals per game 1.07

45 Bob Scott 1961/62 (42 games) goals per game 1.07

44 Bob Scott 1960/61 (47 games) goals per game 0.93

41 Frank Campbell 1957/58 (57 games) goals per game0.72

40 Jack Isherwood 1938/39 (47 games) goals per game 0.85

40 Johnny Pearson 1970/71 (59 games) goals per game 0.68

40 Paul Beck 1989/90 (55 games) goals per game 0.73

Rossendale United F.C. League Record

season	comp	Pl	W	D	L	F	A	Pts	Pos
1898–99	NE Lancs	10	4	2	4	16	18	10	
1898–99	Comb	17	2	4	11	13	56	8	15/15
1899–1900	Central Lancs	16	12	0	4	37	26	24	1/9
1900–01	Central Lancs	18	8	3	7	47	28	19	5/10
1901–02	Comb	34	13	5	16	62	89	31	10/18
1902–03	Comb	34	10	6	18	49	87	26	15/18
1903–04	Comb 1	34	13	7	14	45	57	33	10/18
1904–05	Comb 1	34	12	8	14	54	68	32	13/18
1905–06	Comb 1	38	14	8	16	68	73	36	12/20
1906–07	Comb 1	38	13	10	15	71	70	36	13/20
1907–08	Comb 1	38	18	7	13	69	64	43	5/20
1908–09	Comb 1	38	11	7	20	58	94	29	18/20
1909–10	Comb 2	38	21	4	13	105	69	46	6/20

season	comp	Pl	W	D	L	F	A	Pts	Pos
1910–11	Comb 2	38	19	7	12	124	64	45	7/20
1911–12	Comb 1	32	12	9	11	58	48	33	8/17
1912–13	Comb 1	34	8	7	19	63	105	23	17/18
1913–14	Comb2	34	19	4	11	84	42	42	3/18
1914–15	Comb 1	32	11	0	21	42	64	22	15/17
1919–20	Comb	34	16	3	15	64	71	35	10/18
1920–21	Comb	34	10	5	19	52	76	25	14/18
1921–22	Comb	34	13	8	13	66	51	34	10/18
1922–23	Comb	34	19	3	12	85	55	41	5/18
1923–24	Comb	38	18	8	12	69	56	44	5/20
1924–25	Comb	36	16	9	11	78	67	41	6/19
1925–26	Comb	38	23	4	11	119	89	50	3/20
1926–27	Comb	38	27	6	5	129	65	60	1/20
1927–28	Comb	38	21	7	10	110	60	49	5/20
1928–29	Comb	38	23	4	11	126	74	50	3/20
1929–30	Comb	38	18	7	13	83	82	43	8/20
1930–31	Comb	38	15	6	17	83	99	37	15/20
1931–32	Comb	36	18	6	12	86	74	42	6/19
1932–33	Comb	38	10	11	17	65	89	31	15/20
1933–34	Comb	38	13	6	19	70	98	32	14/20
1934–35	Comb	38	22	6	10	103	65	50	5/20
1935–36	Comb	40	10	9	21	77	108	29	19/21
1936–37	Comb	40	11	6	23	81	134	28	19/21
1937–38	Comb	42	18	7	17	74	73	43	9/22
1938–39	Comb	42	19	12	11	95	50	50	6/22
1945–46	Comb	22	9	4	9	53	47	22	6/12
1946–47	Comb	42	11	10	21	76	113	32	20/22
1947–48	Comb 1	42	11	12	19	80	90	34	15/22
1948–49	Comb 1	42	17	8	17	85	78	42	12/22
1949–50	Comb 1	42	13	8	21	73	85	34	18/22
1950–51	Comb 1	42	13	7	22	63	102	33	19/22
1951–52	Comb 1	42	13	5	24	77	95	31	20/22
1952–53	Comb 1	42	16	7	19	84	92	39	14/22
1953–54	Comb 1	40	14	8	18	87	89	36	13/21
1954–55	Comb 1	42	24	6	12	123	84	54	2/22
1955–56	Comb 1	38	8	9	21	61	89	25	19/20
1956–57	Comb 2	34	25	3	6	111	34	53	1/18
1957–58	Comb 1	42	19	10	13	104	88	48	8/22
1958–59	Comb 1	42	16	5	21	88	89	37	16/22

season	comp	Pl	W	D	L	F	A	Pts	Pos
1959–60	Comb 1	42	21	7	14	116	95	49	5/22
1960–61	Comb 1	42	13	7	22	92	139	33	16/22
1961–62	Comb 1	42	22	6	14	114	89	50	6/22
1962–63	Comb 1	42	17	6	19	103	138	40	14/22
1963–64	Comb 1	42	12	9	21	70	114	33	16/22
1964–65	Comb 1	42	13	6	23	75	114	32	18/22
1965–66	Comb 1	42	9	9	24	48	97	27	18/22
1966–67	Comb 1	42	12	8	22	64	90	32	18/22
1967–68	Comb 1	42	6	6	30	50	115	18	22/22
1968–69	Comb	42	16	8	18	68	83	40	13/22
1969–70	Comb	38	22	4	12	96	50	48	7/20
1970–71	Ches	42	28	11	3	84	39	67	1/22
1971–72	Ches	42	26	5	11	90	65	57	2/22
1972–73	Ches	42	21	9	12	62	40	51	5/22
1973–74	Ches	42	29	6	7	87	39	64	2/22
1974–75	Ches	42	17	13	12	77	64	47	8/22
1975–76	Ches	42	17	9	16	69	62	43	11/22
1976–77	Ches	42	9	10	23	48	85	28	20/22
1977–78	Ches	42	11	4	27	51	110	24	20/22
1978–79	Ches 1	42	11	6	25	51	108	28	19/22
1979–80	Ches 1	38	12	12	14	48	73	36	11/20
1980–81	Ches 1	38	9	12	17	49	69	30	15/20
1981–82	Ches 1	38	18	10	10	62	44	46	5/20
1982–83	Nwc 2	38	15	10	13	75	68	40	8/20
1983–84	Nwc 2	34	10	6	18	53	84	26	15/18
1984–85	Nwc 2	34	10	9	15	51	53	29	14/18
1985–86	Nwc 2	34	20	8	6	81	36	48	2/18
1986–87	Nwc 1	38	14	11	13	66	59	39	10/20
1987–88	Nwc 1	34	24	7	3	68	23	55	2/18
1988–89	Nwc 1	34	24	8	2	84	27	56	1/18
1989–90	Npl1	42	15	9	18	73	69	54	13/22
1990–91	Npl1	42	12	13	17	66	67	48*	15/22
1991–92	Npl1	42	9	11	22	61	90	38	19/22
1992–93	Npl1	40	5	5	30	50	126	20	21/21
1993–94	Nwc 1	42	25	9	8	76	46	84	2/22
1994–95	Nwc 1	42	12	11	19	60	82	47	18/22
1995–96	Nwc 1	42	6	10	26	32	114	28	21/22
1996–97	Nwc 1	42	11	9	22	61	90	38	17/22
1997–98	Nwc 1	42	15	6	21	61	80	51	13/22

season	comp	Pl	W	D	L	F	A	Pts	Pos
1998–99	Nwc 1	40	14	5	21	59	81	47	14/21
1999–00	Nwc 1	42	23	9	10	77	46	78	5/22
2000–01	Nwc 1	42	29	5	8	114	44	92	1/22
2001–02	Npl1	42	17	10	15	69	58	61	9/22
2002–03	Npl1	42	12	5	25	58	88	41	18/22
2003–04	Npl1	42	13	12	17	53	62	51	15/22
2004–05	Npl1	42	10	10	22	64	87	40	21/22
2005–06	Npl1	42	12	17	13	58	67	53	15/22
2006–07	Npl1N	46	21	7	18	64	59	70	9/22
2007–08	Npl1N	42	16	11	15	66	74	59	9/18
2008–09	Npl1N	40	8	10	22	53	83	34	21/21
2009–10	Npl1N	42	6	7	29	38	94	25	22/22
2010–11	NwcP	42	6	11	25	63	106	28*	21/22
Totals		3981	1554	777	1650	7473	7818	4175	

*Indicate point deducted for breach of rules

War time record

season	Comp	Pl	W	D	L	F	A	Pts	Pos
1915–16	Comb N	18	8	3	7	41	30	19	4/10
1915–16	Supp N	12	4	1	7	21	33	9	6/7
1939–40	Comb	18	10	1	7	56	39	21	3/10
1940–41	Man	27	19	1	7	95	51	39	2/8
1941–42	Comb	18	12	0	6	68	31	24	4/10
1942–43	Comb	10	6	0	4	38	24	12	3/6
1943–44	Comb	12	9	0	3	34	16	18	1/7

Captain Bob Woods and Chairman Billy Holden with the Cheshire League trophy and the rest of the successful 1971 squad. Manager Les Rigby is on the far right.

The author far right back row in his one and only appearance for Rossendale United Reserves in 1989.

Back row: Paul Round (manager), Alex Binnie, Russell Procter, Alan Livesey, John Parrott, Liam Boardman, Steve Walker, Dave Rogan.

Front row: Linton James, Andy Hornsby, Ged Walsh, Brent Peter(assistant manager), Mark Rawstron, Chris Ireland.

The Author David Rogan, a Rossy lad born and bred is a life long Rossendale United fan who over the years acted as Secretary, reserve team secretary, Programme editor and was one of the few volunteers who was there at the end ensuring the club completed the 2010 –11 season.